JENNIFER PARKER

McBUSTED

The Story of the World's Biggest Superband

SIMON &
SCHUSTER

London · New York · Sydney · Toronto · New Delhi

A CBS COMPANY

First published in Great Britain by Simon & Schuster UK Ltd, 2014
A CBS COMPANY

3 5 7 9 10 8 6 4 2

Simon & Schuster UK Ltd
1st Floor
222 Gray's Inn Road
London WC1X 8HB

www.simonandschuster.co.uk

Simon & Schuster Australia, Sydney
Simon & Schuster India, New Delhi

A CIP catalogue record for this book is available from the British Library

ISBN: 978-1-47114-065-5
ISBN: 978-1-47114-067-9 (ebook)

Typeset in the UK by M Rules
Printed and bound by CPI Group (UK) Ltd, Croydon, CR0 4YY

For JB
Thank you for the music

CONTENTS

PROLOGUE

Friday, 14 January 2005, wasn't a particularly chilly day – it was a mild 8 degrees Celsius on the bustling London streets outside – but the atmosphere inside the stunned press-conference room at the Soho Hotel was as cold as ice. Amid a cacophony of calls from the waiting journalists and a blizzard of camera flashes, the three men hurriedly made their way from the room, having just delivered the worst news of two of their young lives.

The door closed behind them. For the first time in three years, there was only silence. How to find the words to say goodbye?

How to find the words to say goodbye?

They didn't even try. Matt and James made their way, glumly, to the car park. It was grey concrete all around, as gloomy and as hard and unforgiving as the choices now before them. They faced each other, the end of everything written in the slope of their downturned necks, in their downcast eyes.

They shook hands, formally, but almost immediately Matt flicked his long, dark fringe – styled just on the one side in the emo fashion – out of his eyeliner-ringed eyes and pulled James into a massive hug. This wasn't the time for being cool.

This was the end.

James hugged him back, hard. He'd never thought it would finish like this. He pulled his baseball cap down firmly over his eyes, and slipped silently into the waiting car. The door slammed, echoing around the cavernous car park, and the car drove off. Matt couldn't even bear to watch the tail-lights fade away.

Which was why he was so surprised when he heard James call his name at the top of his voice.

'*Matt!*'

His bandmate ran up to him, the car in which he was supposed to be sitting somehow still in sight in the distance, travelling at speed – and yet James was very much here, now, panting and desperate, and clutching a tour programme in his hand. Matt struggled to compute what he was seeing, his forehead furrowed with the effort. James grabbed him and held his arms tight.

'We've got to go back!' he declared vehemently.

'Back?' echoed Matt. 'Back where?'

James paused for a moment – and then delivered the line to end all lines.

'Back – to the future!'

ONE

Loser Kid

L ondon, 1999. It was an audition room much like any other. Eager hopefuls thronged the corridors, practising scales with gusto and wondering whether today of all days was going to be their lucky one. It was wintertime, and it was the age of the boy band: Westlife, Five and the Backstreet Boys were all riding high in the charts. Each of the young lads waiting nervously in that London studio hoped desperately that he, too, could emulate their success by landing a place in this brand-new band.

One of them was sixteen-year-old James Bourne. He'd brought his guitar with him, as always, and plucked out a melody absent-mindedly as he waited his turn to perform – perhaps finding the chords of 'I Want It That Way' by the Backstreet Boys, which had hit number one back in May, a song from Green Day's classic album *Dookie*, or something by his idol Michael Jackson.

Michael Jackson was the reason he was here, really. When James had discovered him, aged six, thanks to a tip-off in the lyric of a Bart Simpson record, it was a life-changing moment. Before then, he hadn't had music in his life; though, according to his mum, he'd had a rather maddening habit of bursting into song in his pushchair as a toddler.

Discovering Michael Jackson changed everything. Everything. *Dangerous*, *Bad* – these albums became his cornerstones, and, after seeing Jackson live at Wembley, James had only one ambition in life: he was going to learn to play Michael Jackson songs if it killed him.

It very nearly did. James was a determined child, having inherited his father's can-do attitude, which had seen Peter Bourne succeed as a self-made man running his own sales business. When James was offered the chance to learn an instrument at his preparatory school, Alleyn Court in Southend-on-Sea, he grabbed the guitar with both hands and played it till his fingers bled – literally.

He grabbed the guitar with both hands and played it till his fingers bled

His perseverance paid off. It may have taken a few years, but he got there in the end; and discovered a talent not only for playing Michael Jackson songs but for writing music, too. And he loved performing. Aged ten, he'd taken part in a local production of the musical *Oliver!* and found that, like the lead character, he wanted more. An open audition for the West End production followed, and James had spent two happy years living it up at the

London Palladium, playing first Kipper in Fagin's gang, and then the starring role of Oliver himself.

But you can't remain a child star for ever, and James didn't want to. As he'd grown up, his music tastes had broadened too: he loved Green Day, and the cheekiness of Robbie Williams's lyrics. Soon, he'd formed his own band, Sic Puppy, and was writing original material. Aged thirteen, at his new school, the Morgan Academy of Performing Arts, he'd met an amazing girl, an aspiring actress called Kara Tointon, who was now his girlfriend. Life was pretty good – and he was hoping this audition was going to make it even better.

Soon enough, James was called in to do his best. He went nervously into the audition room, barely noticing a brown-haired boy, also with a guitar, who was waiting his turn, too. All his attention was focused on the powers-that-be who were seated behind the desk. One of them was a confident American man by the name of Richard Rashman, of Prestige Management.

Little did James know it, but that man was about to change his life.

But not by casting him in this particular pop band. James was turned down. He got a no.

So did the brown-haired boy.

Sometimes, when one door closes, an even better one opens.

A little over a year later, in early 2001, there was a knock on the door of James's parents' house in Southend. James, hearing it, started to make his way downstairs from the top-floor bedroom he shared with his brother Nick, who was eighteen months younger than he was. They were very different, but they got on like a house on fire. The younger of James's brothers, Chris, was more like him, but, with a decade between them in age, it would be a few years yet before they could make music together. Sister Melissa, three years older than Chris, completed the Bourne siblings.

James pulled open the door. He was dressed casually in a pair of pale corduroy trousers and a Mambo T-shirt, with a surfer-style cap balanced on his thick blond hair – all likely sourced from his favourite Southend surf shop, Exile. He was seventeen years old, and currently attending college, studying a music-technology course that was teaching him how to produce his own tracks. In his spare time, he wrote songs – and dreamed of the day when he could quit college and join a band. Maybe, just maybe, the person who had knocked on the door would be the answer to his prayers.

But the person on his doorstep was too busy taking in the impressive façade of the huge house with the stunning sea view to answer to anything, even his name – Matt Willis or, as he was more commonly known then, Mathew Sargeant, the surname being that of his mother's new husband, Brian. Matt grew up on the wrong side of the tracks in Molesey (a town in well-to-do Surrey, but Matt lived in the dodgy bit), where his mum Linda worked in pubs and his dad, Kevin Willis, made a living working in a factory. Linda and Kevin had met in a working men's club in the 1970s, had Matt's brother, Darren, in 1981, and then Matt came along in May 1983. Money was tight – which made James's house such an eye-opener to the seventeen-year-old Matt – but love was plentiful, both from his parents, even after they split up when Matt was three years old, and from his extended family. One of his earliest memories was of his aunt and uncle playing him

Elvis videos; something about the charismatic swagger, musical talent and sheer star quality of the King of Rock and Roll had him hooked, though it would be years before he acted on his natural affinity for showmanship.

In the meantime, there were rules to be broken and games to be played. Matt was a mischief maker from the word go; by the time he was ten he had broken twenty-eight bones in his body, mostly from dangerous jumps from trees and high walls. Not for nothing was his mum's nickname for him 'Fidget'. He would fidget in lessons, too, which led to his leaving one school for another, a reputation as a troublemaker trailing in his wake.

Matt was a mischief maker from the word go

It was a couple of other well-known troublemakers who would open the door to a whole new life for him, though. One night, Matt and his family were down the pub and there was a karaoke night on. His mum urged him to take the mic, having never heard him sing before. Her request was for Marti Pellow and the dulcet tones of Wet Wet Wet's 'Love Is All Around', but Matt was never one to follow instructions. Instead, he performed the Gallagher brothers' 'Don't Look Back in Anger', his voice rasping impressively above the din in the pub, making people pay attention. Afterwards, a local songwriter came up to Matt and asked him to record one of the writer's songs for him; that done, without Matt's knowledge, he sent the demo to the Sylvia Young Theatre School, where there was a scholarship up for grabs.

The Sylvia Young Theatre School had a reputation that had reached even the working-class streets of Molesey – though it didn't necessarily have alumni that would appeal to the rebellious young Mathew Sargeant. Spice Girl Emma Bunton and pop princess Billie Piper were both former students, it wasn't quite the rock roots that Matt was starting to cultivate. He had a passion for Green Day by then, and a band of his own called Sabotage, who diligently covered Green Day songs – albeit without ever performing a single gig. Besides which, Sylvia Young was based in Marylebone, London, and was an independent fee-paying school. There was no way someone like Matt could afford to go there.

Encouraged by his mum, he nonetheless went to the audition that the songwriter had secured for him. But it was to no avail: the scholarship went elsewhere. Then, unexpectedly, Sylvia Young herself phoned the family and made them a generous offer: if Matt agreed to go on her agency books – through which he could audition for TV shows, adverts and the like – he could pay his school fees using his earnings. It was an extraordinary opportunity, and one that Matt embraced with all the enthusiasm a cool dude with a passion for rock can visibly demonstrate.

As it happened, his cool vibe stood him in good stead, landing him lots of jobs to help pay his way through theatre school – even if he did always end up cast as the drug dealer in programmes such as *Casualty* and *The Bill*. His success enabled him to knuckle down and enjoy his schooldays – in more ways than one. With a ratio of five boys to twenty-four girls in his class, Matt had a field day breaking hearts, including that of a certain Amy Winehouse, an aspiring singer who fancied him something rotten. Matt,

Matt had a field day breaking hearts

however, seemed to have eyes only for his dance teacher, the elfin-faced Ms Michelle Blair, though his affections were never requited.

But music was his first love, and in March 2000, not long after that failed band audition for Prestige Management, an album that changed his life was released in the UK: Blink-182's *Enema of the State*, which boasted class-act tracks such as 'All the Small Things' and 'Adam's Song' – iconic anthems about authentic adolescent life. Matt had found what he wanted to do for the rest of his life: form a band and make music. Really, he wanted to be in Blink-182, but it looked as if they were doing pretty well without him. So now his only problem was finding the ideal bandmates with whom he could make his dreams come true. But how was he going to find them among his high-kicking, jazz-handing peers at Sylvia Young?

Richard Rashman was the answer. Prestige Management's Rashman had been impressed with both James and Matt at that unsuccessful audition in winter 1999. While neither had been right for that band, he could see they both had talent, and encouraged them to keep at it, particularly with their songwriting. He stayed in touch with them both throughout that following year of 2000, and eventually had the brainwave of connecting them with each other. And so it came to be that early in 2001, Matt Willis stood on the doorstep of James Bourne's house in Southend, wondering if they might just be able to make some music together.

'Come in,' said James, and he opened the door wide.

He led Matt into his parents' dining room, where a piano was set up next to an imposing eight-track home recording studio. James, like Matt, was a jobbing actor from time to time and had just blown almost his entire £2,000 fee from a recent job on the new equipment. Matt couldn't help but be impressed with the set-up.

And he was even more impressed when James started playing him some of the tracks he'd been working on, including an original song called 'Living Without Your Love'. The two boys had recognised each other a bit when James had first opened the door, perhaps from that failed band audition, but also from other gigs and acting auditions. Now, Matt recognised a kindred spirit.

There were some other introductions to make. James had just recently started working with a couple of other Rashman-connected musicians: Ki Fitzgerald, who lived in Kent, and Owen Doyle, from Birmingham. The four of them decided to try to work together as a band, at first under the somewhat dubious name of the Termites. Rashman kept a close eye on their burgeoning progress and, on 15 March 2001, each of the boys signed a management deal with Prestige. It was an exciting time, particularly when, the very next day, the band went in for a meeting with Sony. It didn't come to anything, but the executive they saw was encouraging and it gave them hope that, with a bit of hard work, they might just have something.

Matt and James hit it off immediately. They literally just sat down together and started writing songs; their partnership came that naturally. The first song they wrote together was a little ballad called 'Sleeping with the Light On', but others soon followed over the next few months. 'Living Without Your Love' evolved into a track called 'Psycho Girl'. And when they penned

'What I Go to School For', about Matt's crush on his dance instructor at Sylvia Young, Ms Blair – though they changed her name to Miss Mackenzie – they knew they had something really special. So special, in fact, that James found the courage to quit his college course at Easter, even without a firm record deal in place. It was a brave step, but he believed in both himself and in the music.

The Termites was not a band name that you could believe in, though, and all four members were keen to change it. Rumours abound about where the name 'Busted' came from: some say it was Rashman, others the boys themselves, others still that it was the former Spice Girl Geri Halliwell who coined it, when she mispronounced the name 'Buster' as 'Busted' after Ki's sister had called her on an MTV phone-in, to tell her about her brother's new band. However it came about, from April 2001, 'Busted' was the name of the band – and they were on their way.

James wasn't the only one taking the band seriously. From summer 2001, Matt pretty much moved into James's family home in Southend in order to focus on the music they were making; at first just crashing on James's bedroom floor – until he was there so often that Peter and Maria Bourne insisted on getting him a proper bed. He and James would write and sing together all the time, gathered round the piano in the downstairs dining room. As well as honing the songs they'd already written – with James sharing his enthusiasm for Backstreet Boys' pop classics – they were still coming up with original material too. One day, they channelled James's obsessive love of the 1985 film *Back to the Future* into musical form with a track called 'Year 3000'.

Matt became like a new Bourne brother to Chris, Melissa and

Nick, and, when Nick received his GCSE exam results during that golden summer, Matt assumed responsibility for teaching him how to celebrate. Nick later told journalist Peter Robinson, '[Matt] had a massive party for me in my house. He poured loads of different things in a jug and we drank it. The first time I ever got drunk was with Matt.'

With James, too, Matt was fond of a bevy or two. In the book *Busted*, he recalls of that summer, 'I think to be honest that James and I were pissed almost all the time.' They were going out to the local student union bars in Southend and enjoying the cheap beer – which made a nice change for Matt, who was used to paying over the odds to opportunists who saw a chance to exploit underage drinkers. He told *Digital Spy* in 2006 about his experiences as a teenager in Surrey: 'You'd meet this one person, who'd have his car, and in his boot were loads of bottles of cider, and they'd be like seven pounds each. Seven pounds for a bottle of cider! Cost him three pounds, but he'd be like, "I'm eighteen, you're twelve, what are you going to do about it?"' Matt smoked, too – cigarettes and cannabis, which he'd started taking at the age of thirteen – yet this haze of booze and drugs certainly didn't seem to hinder his creativity. In fact, his and James's partnership just seemed to get better and better.

In August 2001, Busted stepped up to their biggest challenge yet: recording a demo at a London studio. The four boys decamped to the capital to take up temporary residence at the

I think to be honest that James and I were pissed almost all the time

InterContinental hotel on Park Lane. As they walked through the grand lobby, with its cool marble floor reflecting the shimmering chandeliers above, they allowed themselves to dream that maybe one day they would belong in this luxury world. All it needed was for the demo to work; all they needed was a break.

They couldn't wait to hear the finished tracks.

They waited . . . and waited. August turned to September, and there was still no sign of the finished demo tapes. The boys had been signed to Prestige since March; they'd been working together since January; and they still felt no further forward than at the start of the year. James in particular – who had broken up with his beloved Kara and was worried that he'd quit college for what seemed to be a floundering band – felt the disappointment sharply. He wrote in *Busted* that, before his eighteenth birthday in September 2001, 'It suddenly struck me that I had nothing . . . I was pinning everything on a band that would probably never even get off the ground. I had a terrible, sinking feeling.' He continued:

Am I stupid to dream that this band is going to take off?

One night, when my anxiety became too much to bear, I sat down with my mum and we tried to find the answers to my problems. It had just gone 11 p.m. and I asked my mum, 'Am I stupid to dream that this band is going to take off?' She looked at me, and grasped my hand, and answered, 'It'll happen, James. You'll make it happen.'

James started to wonder what more he could do to make the band succeed; and he began to think that maybe Richard Rashman wasn't the man to make it happen for him. They'd had a crisis meeting in June about the lack of progress, which had prompted the demo recordings, but now they were back at square one – and still with nothing to show for all the months of hard work.

Cracks were beginning to show within the band, though. Matt and James, always a tight unit, longed to explore the rock-oriented route that they loved in bands such as Blink-182 and Green Day, but Owen hankered after a more traditional boy-band format. The situation was untenable. Something had to give.

On Wednesday, 3 October 2001, the boys faxed Rashman to terminate their management agreement with him. He didn't feel the sacking was justified and immediately phoned them to discuss the matter. Nothing was resolved that day but, on the Thursday, Rashman caught up with Matt on his mobile, as he was travelling to Southend to see James. Matt told him that he didn't want to continue working with Owen and Ki any more, but he was still interested in being represented by Rashman. Meanwhile, in Southend, Rashman's associate, the talented musician and artist manager Matthew 'Fletch' Fletcher, called on James to discuss the falling-out too.

Fletch and James had known each other for a while by this time. The two of them had written music together and James respected Fletch's opinion. If Fletch thought it was worthwhile giving Rashman another go, it was. Simple as that. Matt and James discussed it together and told Rashman that they were interested in being represented by him as a twosome only. They wanted to try working together to create something new, rather than continuing with the old band. On Monday, 8 October, the old Busted disbanded.

Yet James and Matt didn't want to be just a two-piece. How many successful male double acts were there? The Everly Brothers? Wham? PJ and Duncan? None of them were quite as cool as Blink-182. A double act wouldn't give them the rock edge they were yearning for.

There was only one thing for it. They'd have to audition for new members of the band. A tiny ad was taken out in the hallowed pages of the *New Musical Express* (*NME*) and the *Stage* that very same month. Fletch, Rashman, James and Matt were on the hunt for the boys' perfect match. And there was one young man who was hoping he was just what they were looking for.

His name was Tom Fletcher, and he was just about as nervous as you could be before an audition, even though he was actually extremely experienced for one of so few years – he'd just turned sixteen that past July. Tom was born in 1985 into a house full of music: his dad Bob played guitar and sang in a covers band, and Tom first picked up a guitar at the age of five. Later, he learned piano, too, and the first track he mastered was a Backstreet Boys song. His mum, Debbie, worked in a video store when Tom was a kid, prompting a lifelong love of movies in her son; she then became a teaching assistant while he was still at school. Both his parents certainly assisted Tom and his younger sister Carrie in anything they wanted to do. And what Tom wanted to do, more than anything, was perform – just like Michael Jackson, who was his absolute idol.

A stint of sessions at the Saturday-morning performing-arts

school Stagecoach saw him spotted by a teacher at a local full-time theatre school, and from there Tom moved on to a place he felt he truly could call home: the Sylvia Young Theatre School. Like the rest of the kids there, he went out regularly to audition for shows, and, when he was ten, a big one came up: *Oliver!* in the West End. Guess what? He first landed the part of Kipper – and then went on to play the lead role of Oliver. He must have missed James by just a couple of years.

Sylvia Young certainly gave him the time of his life – and introduced him to a girl he was pretty sure was the love of his life, too. One morning in assembly, when he was thirteen, a pretty new girl with Italian good looks walked into the school hall and lit up his world. Fate was on his side: her surname was Falcone, which meant the teacher directed her to sit next to Mr Fletcher. She walked over and knocked him for six with a megawatt smile.

'Hi, I'm Giovanna, but you can call me Gi.'

Tom didn't miss a beat. 'Hi, I'm Tom, but you can call me T.'

That was the start of it, but it was nowhere near the end. Going out by the end of that fateful day, they broke up two days later, got back together, and then broke up again when Tom's time at Sylvia Young's came to an end in the summer of 2001. Waiting nervously outside the audition room at the Pineapple Dance Studios in Covent Garden that October morning, Tom wondered what Gi would say to him now. She always seemed to be able to inspire him. But, for the moment at least, she wasn't his to call on. He was going to have to win this one by himself.

He fidgeted with his audition number, 35, which was pinned to his loose-fitting grey sweatshirt, and tweaked his slickly gelled blond hair. Looking around at the 200-odd musicians who were all clearly there to try their luck, he was somewhat relieved to spot a familiar face from school. It was Matt Willis. He'd been a couple of years ahead of Tom and Tom had always been a bit intimidated by him – Matt was one of the cool kids, a rebel, and cautious Tom was anything but that – but auditions were a great equaliser. They were probably both nervous as hell; it would be good to share the pain.

'Hi, mate, you auditioning?' Tom asked, in a friendly way.

Matt shook his head, his hair – gelled into crazy spikes and strobed with one blond streak on the right-hand side – not moving an inch. 'No, I'm in the band.'

Tom's heart sank as the confident Matt strode away, his eyes coolly assessing the auditionees lining the corridor, as far away from Tom as he had been in school. Matt wasn't going to want someone like Tom in his band. I might as well go home, thought Tom. I'm not getting in this.

Tom had always been a bit intimidated by Matt

It was his mum who persuaded him to stay. And, as the clock hit 10.30 a.m., the tryouts began. Tom walked into the audition room. There were Fletch and Rashman, from the band's management – they already had management, how cool was that? – and a kid he didn't know, who introduced himself as James Bourne. Then there was Matt. Tom swallowed hard, and decided to put his insecurities to one side. He slung his black-and-grey guitar strap around his neck and went for it. He'd prepared Garth Brooks's 'The Dance' – a moody, atmospheric country ballad – and also BBMak's 'Back Here'. He got the chance to show off his piano skills, too, when another boy needed some accompaniment for his audition: Tom confidently played a Backstreet Boys track as his rival crooned his heart out. By the end of the day, Tom was down to the last four.

But he had some hot competition in that final four, most notably from six-foot-two guitarist Charlie Simpson. Tom didn't know it at that stage, but, from the moment Fletch had seen Charlie coming through the door, he was a frontrunner. As James recalled in *Busted*, 'Fletch came up to us at the start and said, "I've just seen this guy at the door. He's exactly what we need."'

> I've just seen this guy at the door. He's exactly what we need

And Charlie certainly fitted the bill. As well as being tall, he had model good looks to die for, with chiselled cheekbones that could cut through glass and a pair of dark bushy eyebrows that framed his beautiful brown eyes perfectly. (He was, in fact, soon to be signed to the top modelling agency Models 1, which represented the supermodels Twiggy and Linda Evangelista, among others.) That day, he was wearing flared blue jeans and a light-blue shirt with a sharp collar, with his audition number, 27, pinned to his chest. He looked hot. And he soon proved he wasn't just a pretty face. As well as being a talented vocalist, with a rocky drawl of a voice which sounded iconic from the moment he opened his mouth, he could play the guitar like a dream – and the drums as well. As Matt put it in *Busted*, 'We thought he'd been sent from heaven.'

Not quite heaven – but not far off. Charlie was a sixteen-year-old student at the very grand Uppingham School in Rutland, an exclusive boarding school, which was, at that time, for boys only, and which had been founded in 1584. It boasted the kind of plush grounds that would have blown Matt's mind, had he known about them. The golden stone of the main school house was dotted with historic mullioned windows, and Uppingham also had its own private Victorian-era chapel and 120 acres of land. Fees in 2014 for a single term ran to over £10,000.

But, blessed though Charlie was with financial security, money didn't rock his world. Music did. From the age of seven, he'd been a rock-music nut, taking inspiration from his older brothers Will and Edd, who introduced him to bands such as Metallica and Guns N' Roses. On 7 June 1995 – his tenth birthday – he was given his first electric guitar, and he never looked back. Several bands followed: his first, Natural Disasters, was formed when he was twelve, but he also played in Fubar, Manhole and Spleen. At Uppingham, he met an inspirational music teacher, Alexis French, who urged him to follow his dreams, telling Charlie, 'You've got what it takes. Forget school and go for it.'

Which was how he found himself down to the last four in the auditions for the final places in Busted; not that he knew at that stage what the band were called. The name was not revealed till a second audition a couple of days later, when Tom, Charlie and the others joined Matt, James and the management at the InterContinental on Park Lane. Matt and James played the boys 'What I Go to School For', and the hopefuls took turns singing it with them. Tom felt brave enough to showcase one of his own tracks, 'I'm in Love with a Whore'. It wasn't quite McCartney-level brilliance, but it made everyone laugh, and Tom started to think that he might be in with a chance – even more so when he and James got chatting and realised that, as well as sharing a love of Michael Jackson and *Back to the Future*, and the lead role in *Oliver!* in the West End, they'd actually worked on some other shows together when they were much, much younger. Surely it must be fate?

It was. That same night, Tom and Charlie got a phone call from Richard Rashman. They were in the band. Could they come down to the studio the following week?

As October 2001 drew to a close, the new Busted – James Bourne, Matt Willis, Charlie Simpson and Tom Fletcher – met in a recording studio in London to start work on the rest of their lives.

Afterwards, the band headed to a fast-food restaurant to celebrate. They were just four teenagers, after all. Tom remembered that day clearly in the ITV documentary *Fearne and McBusted*: 'We all went to Burger King afterwards and were like, "This is it, we're a band, this is the band." And we swapped phone numbers with each other, and I was like, "These are my bandmates, it's really cool." I said goodbye to Charlie on the Tube and I was like, "See you around, bandmate."'

Tom headed home and helped his family prepare for a huge Hallowe'en party they were hosting in the next day or so. Tom had told everyone his news, so, when the party started, all the guests were high-fiving him as he excitedly made his way through the crowd. In the midst of all this celebration, the phone rang. It was Richard Rashman.

Tom took the call upstairs. He recalled the momentous phone conversation in the McFly book *Unsaid Things*, and how

Rashman's American drawl had hammered home each word: 'Hello, Tom. So we've been talking . . . and we've decided to keep the band as a trio. So we're really sorry, but we're keeping it as Matt, Charlie and James. You're not going to be in the band.'

Later, on the TV music channel The Vault, Matt would try to explain the situation: 'Tom was never really necessarily in the band; we were trying things out and Tom was around at that period of time. I don't think he was ever truly . . . I think our management had told him he was in the band but *we* had never told him he was in the band. It was for like one day, and then he suddenly wasn't – which is awful.'

'Awful' didn't really cover it. Tom sat with the phone cradled against his ear. Rashman was still talking, trying to soften the blow by complimenting Tom's songwriting and saying how he wanted to stay in touch, but Tom knew it was just lip service. He hung up the phone and sat there in his bedroom, the noise of the Hallowe'en party coming up through the floor.

This was the worst trick-or-treat ever. Tom sat as still as a statue, as the ghosts of his dreams floated far, far away.

TWO

Can't Break Through

Click!
  The camera flash fired as the shot was taken, momentarily blinding the three boys, who were crouched in an awkward pose in the bathroom of their hotel room. It was the new Busted's first ever photoshoot, and it was a DIY job with a disposable camera. They'd figured the lighting was better in the loo, but, when the results came back from Snappy Snaps, even they had to admit that their music was clearly superior to their photography skills.

Yet the dodgy snaps couldn't dent their enthusiasm for working together. Matt, in particular, was over the moon about the line-up, saying in *Busted*, 'Charlie's audition was perfect, and I still think to this day [July 2003] that if he hadn't been at that audition, we wouldn't have accepted anyone else.' Eat your heart out, Tom Fletcher.

If Charlie hadn't been at that audition, we wouldn't have accepted anyone else

The new band were professional from the start, that first photoshoot aside. Their first job was to get a demo together that they could send to record companies, so Matt, Charlie and James visited Steve Robson's studio to lay down some tracks, recording 'What I Go to School For', 'Psycho Girl' and another song called 'She Knows'. Rashman's plan was to take them round the record companies in January 2002 – but, unexpectedly, they found they had strong interest from a leading A&R man well before then.

Robson's manager, Sarah Vaughan, was at that time also an A&R administrator for the record label BMG, headed by Simon Cowell, who was just starting to make headlines of his own as a 'Mr Nasty' talent judge on ITV's *Pop Idol*, which debuted to the British viewing public on 6 October 2001. By the time Sarah put in a request for Cowell to get an early look at the new group – a request Rashman granted – he was entertaining up to 7.5 million viewers every week with his caustic comments and unforgettable feedback. This was a man who was notoriously not easy to impress. The boys had a tough task ahead of them.

Their fate was out of their hands as Cowell took the unfinished demo to listen to. Their spirits soared when the A&R exec told Rashman to bring the guys in to see him in January. He was seriously interested, and wanted a first look once the band had been together for longer than two weeks.

The two-week mark since Busted's formation prompted

Rashman to put in another call. He'd been sincere about encouraging Tom Fletcher with his songwriting, and now followed up on his promise to stay in touch. He suggested a meeting, for the very next day, so Tom could play him the songs that Rashman presumed he'd been working on over the past fortnight. Tom, who'd thought Rashman had been kidding when he'd told him during that horrific phone call that it would be good to see him again in a few weeks' time, utterly panicked.

How to rustle up two weeks' worth of songs in twenty-four hours, particularly when the best song you'd written to date was 'I'm in Love with a Whore'? It wasn't as if the past two weeks had been filled with song-quality life experiences. Tom had spent most of the time moping around the house feeling sorry for himself, occasionally crying himself to sleep at night. Getting into the band had seen his confidence sky-rocket – only for it all to be taken away. He'd gone from feeling as though he could achieve anything to having absolutely nothing. And nothing was definitely what he had when Rashman called and asked to hear his latest songs. What songs?

Still, Tom knew the saying about gift horses and mouths, and he wasn't about to look at this pony in the wrong way. As soon as he hung up the phone, he whipped out his guitar and got cracking. What to write about, what to write about? He had it! 'Hot Chicks Dot Com', about the perils of discovering your mum has a profile on a porn site, was the obvious result, along with some other songs that have since been confined to the mists of time.

His meeting with Fletch and Rashman the next day didn't, unsurprisingly, result in their immediately signing him to a music publishing deal – but they did offer a lot of constructive criticism, and proved to him that they were sincere in believing he had talent. Fletch gave him a tip: listen to hit songs and figure out what makes them such smash hits. Well, that was homework? Tom threw himself into it with gusto, devouring the hits of Blink-182, Green Day and Limp Bizkit, of the Backstreet Boys and Britney Spears, of Lennon and McCartney alike.

The Busted boys were being similarly inspired as they spent the winter rehearsing, writing and recording. *American Pie 2* had hit cinemas that October and the soundtrack was something else. Featuring James and Matt's favourite bands Blink-182 and Green Day, the album also boasted songs by thirteen other artists, and as a whole the record was explosively good. According to Matt in his interview with The Vault channel, 'the whole band changed overnight' after listening to that album.

The whole band changed overnight

It was a time of creative freedom and flexibility. The boys revelled in writing about stuff that happened or mattered to them. Bringing in the humour they so loved in Robbie Williams's songs, and the realism that Matt's other favourite band, Madness, excelled at, the three lads found the songs flying out of them. Charlie came into one writing session with a sad tale of how he'd been blown out by a girl, whom he later named in an interview with *Newsround Showbiz* as Daisy Bell. 'I crashed and burned,' he said dejectedly. James's ears pricked up – what an unusual phrase! The boys already had the beginnings of a song about a cocky girl who totally knew how hot she was, and this narrative tied in perfectly. 'Crash and Burn' was the stomping result of a song. It was immediately added to their demo tape, along with James and Matt's old favourite on the theme of time travel, 'Year 3000'.

Christmas came and went, with the band hoping that Santa was just a few weeks late in delivering the item at the top of their wishlists: a record deal. January 2002 brought such a gift tantalisingly within reach, as Rashman and Fletch set up meetings for the guys with record execs at several companies. First up was the by now super-famous Simon Cowell, who was still riding the *Pop Idol* wave, currently cresting at 10 million viewers and counting, despite the fact that everyone knew squeaky-clean stutterer Gareth Gates was going to win.

Fletch gave a vivid account of their meeting with Cowell in an interview with *HR* magazine: 'We'd been told by a songwriter that if he likes something, he plays it through twice. The guys played [acoustically], then he asked them to play again. Then he put the CD on and I thought, "We've got to be in there."'

Maybe they were, maybe they weren't: Cowell gave nothing away. James recalls of that meeting in *Busted*, '[Cowell] was quite cold before he'd heard our stuff and, as you can imagine, we were expecting the worst from him. Then after he'd heard us play, he waited for five seconds – which seemed like the longest time in the world – and said, "Actually, I really like it."' He put a £1 million record deal on the table.

OMFG! as the boys might say. A £1 million record deal. But the boys didn't jump at it straightaway – choosing the right record label required serious consideration. For the band, it was always about the music, about a

He put a £1 million record deal on the table

long-term career, not making a quick buck; and it was about the band as a unit. Cowell was talking about maybe bringing in some other members, changing the format, switching things about a bit, and the group were not at all sure about his plans. They thought they rocked as they were. Would anyone take them seriously as a trio?

They still had several other companies to go. Next up was Paul Adam – who'd also had his fair share of fame, as part of the judging panel of ITV's *Popstars* – who worked at Island Records, part of Universal. Charlie was hopeful about them, as they'd signed the little-known Belgian indie act dEUS, whom Charlie loved.

It was an unconventional meeting. Paul had just moved offices, and the seating had gone missing in the move, so all six of them – the band, the management and Paul – sat on the floor to chat. Yet that lack of formality suited down-to-earth Busted down to the ground. Paul later recalled of the showcase, 'They performed "What I Go to School For", "Year 3000" and "Crash and Burn". They were such bloody good songwriters and they absolutely blew me away. I wanted to lock the door so they wouldn't escape and go to any other record labels!'

The band had nailed it. With labels now fighting over them, pushing them for a decision, it was a tense time: this decision would impact on the rest of their lives. They went away for a week to think about it, and their managers advised them the best they could. Ultimately, Busted made the call to sign with Island.

Fletch gave this analysis of the dilemma in his *HR* magazine interview: 'Although Simon Cowell is brilliant at pop, we don't think he understands the needs of real musicians. The decision was taken from a management point of view. Universal was where we wanted to go and our lawyers got us a great deal ... The deal Busted signed with Island Records was the second largest in the label's history, second only to U2.'

They were an awfully long way from James's home recording studio in Southend now.

But recording was what was next on the cards. Calling on the services of producers Steve Robson and John McLaughlin, Busted prepared to record their debut self-titled album at the Brick Lane Studios in London.

Now they were a bona fide band with a proper record contract and everything, their domestic circumstances needed looking at sharpish. Happy though Matt was to be sharing a home with the Bournes, he couldn't remain with them for ever, and Southend was an impractical location for London-based activities for both James and Matt, anyway. In February 2002, the band took the plunge and all three lads moved into a flat in Princess Park Manor, an exclusive apartment complex in Friern Barnet in north London. It was an enormous place compared with Matt's childhood home, and the three of them settled in right away.

Built in 1849, with a foundation stone laid by Prince Albert, Princess Park Manor was a gorgeous place for the band's first home. A yellow-brick former mental institution converted into flats, the complex boasted rolling green lawns, fashionably designed luxury apartments and an on-site health-and-fitness club, complete with swimming pool. Not that the lads planned on working out any time soon: aside from the distractions of their new bachelor pad, such as their own table football, a ping-pong table and an enormous TV, they were far too busy. With the record contract officially signed on 5 March 2002, the boys got ready for the most life-changing year of their lives.

Rashman also had some paperwork to finish off in March of that year. On 22 March, Ki and Owen – the original Busted band-mates – signed an agreement regarding the songs that had been written during the former Termites' time together. Ki and Owen took sole ownership of the songs 'She Knows' and 'Who's Your Daddy?'. The rest of the songs were agreed to be James and Matt's. And that, or so they thought, was that.

By summer 2002, a buzz about Busted was unmistakeably in the air. The lads had finished their album, recorded their school-set debut video in May, and even got over the hurdle of 'musical differences' early on in the band's life.

James and Charlie hailed from very different musical backgrounds: James was passionate about the kind of pop smashes penned by Max Martin, who had written global hits such as '. . . Baby One More Time' and 'Quit Playing Games (With My Heart)', while Charlie was much more into out-and-out rock and indie music. Nonetheless, the combination somehow worked. Charlie said of the writing process in *Busted*, 'I had a few arguments with James and Mattie . . . I was stuck in the old indie ethic about "We make our music and if anyone else likes it, that's a bonus."' For a band with a massive record deal and a member like James, who seemed to be able to write songs with mass appeal at the drop of a hat, such an outlook was anathema. James wanted to write songs that lots of people would listen to and enjoy.

Charlie found a way of making the tricky balance of artistic integrity and commercial appeal work for him, though the solution seemed to be a little like bundling stuff into a closet, ramming shut the door and hoping for the best. He commented, 'If I want to be a bit self-indulgent every now and again, I just keep the songs to myself.'

July 2002 found the band at their first Party in the Park for the Prince's Trust, an annual music event held in London's Hyde Park. The band hadn't released a single yet, so they were hanging about, getting known, bigging up that buzz and checking out their soon-to-be competition. It was a rather grey day for July, but that didn't dint the enthusiasm of Matt and James – or the 100,000-strong crowd – as they watched the hottest pop acts of the day perform on the enormous stage, including Blue (whose members included an old Sylvia Young pal of Matt's, Lee Ryan), Atomic Kitten and *Pop Idol* finalists Will Young, Gareth Gates and Darius Danesh; Will had unexpectedly scooped the crown from Gareth in February, and scored the biggest-selling single of the year to date with 'Evergreen'.

Charlie, however, was not at all comfortable in this pop-fest. James recalled in *Busted*, 'Charlie was being hilarious because he decided that he "didn't belong" there because of his indie ethic. In all the early pictures of Charlie with fans he's got a face like thunder.'

Pictures with fans were becoming a more and more frequent occurrence when the boys were out and about – and it was a fan base that grew larger still when the teen-favourite music magazine *Smash Hits* chose to put the group on its front cover that summer – pretty much a first for any band who hadn't yet released any music. The headline was, MEET BUSTED, THEY'RE GOING TO BE BIGGER THAN RIK WALLER!

Meet Busted, They're Going to be Bigger than Rik Waller!

And the song that was going to take them there was 'What I Go to School For'. It had been a unanimous choice for the first single. Matt, who was now known to his legions of fans as 'Mattie Jay', his 'Busted name', remembered the moment they wrote the song in *Busted*: 'We got so excited once we'd finished. I knew at that point that "What I Go to School For" was the first potential hit record we'd written together. I suddenly thought, "Bloody hell, we've really got a chance here."'

The press campaign for the single featured the band's first ever professional photoshoot at the Trocadero in London (a shoot at which Matt's 'Busted gurn' first made an appearance, due to his impossible nerves at having his picture taken); a tour of an acoustic set to all the magazines; and a huge gig for all the media at the swanky Institute of Contemporary Arts in central London, which they decked out to look like a school disco. James's little brother Chris came along and was first in line at the front, cheering them on.

Soon, he would find that pole position fought over by thousands upon thousands of screaming girls.

'What I Go to School For' was a savvy choice for a debut single: the naughty storyline of the song, fancying your teacher, was an instant talking point; the chorus was irrepressibly catchy; and the boys' lyrics asserted them as a fun and funny band who were here to entertain you. Their lexicon had a grown-up slant, too. This wasn't bubblegum pop, but a hybrid between pop and rock that was brand new. The boys' 'dance' moves – high-energy jumps

with their knees tucked in tight as they power-played their guitars – were soon almost as recognisable as Jackson's moonwalk.
Once the record finally hit shops on 26 September 2002, it was an
instant hit; and not just with their teenage fans. *Music Week*
described it as 'unfeasibly catchy, melody-driven pop with attitude', while the music bible *NME* simply went for 'ace'. The
respect of the music press was the cherry on top of an enormous
commercial hit.

Fletch broke the midweek-sales news to Matt while he was
staying at his mum's. The record was on course to debut at
number three; it was a sensation. His mum was out when Matt
got the call, so he had no one with whom to toast the news. He
then did a most un-Matt-like thing: he had a cup of tea to celebrate.

With the first album put to bed, James found he started to have
a bit of time to think about writing new songs again. And he had
a crazy idea about whom he wanted to write them with. He'd
heard from Fletch and Rashman that Tom Fletcher was still in
touch with them, and writing better and better songs with every
week that passed. James had always thought that Tom was very
talented – the decision for him not to join Busted had had nothing
to do with James's appreciation of his songwriting skills – and,
with Tom now having mastered the art of structuring songs,
thanks to Fletch's encouragement, James suggested to his managers that maybe he and Tom could get together to write.

Tom pulled up to James's flash apartment in Princess Park
Manor one evening – and just about managed to pick his jaw up
off the floor at the sight of the new pop star's lavish home.

It had been a lonely few months for Tom. He'd concentrated

on improving his songwriting, and had finally received a nod of approval from the hard-to-please Fletch with a song called 'Hot Date', but, without a band or any bandmates, it was hard to make any real progress. Perhaps this partnership with James might lead somewhere.

Tom slammed the door of his little Fiat Punto and made his way inside. It was eight o'clock in the evening and they had a good couple of hours ahead of them to write some stuff, if the magic happened. James invited him into the bachelor pad and showed him around, chatting nineteen to the dozen; and Tom responded in kind. They literally could not stop talking and laughing, sharing jokes and geeky observations and their passions, like *Back to the Future* and – of course – Michael Jackson. If this was hitting it off, they'd scored a home run.

In James I had found an amazing friend and mentor

Tom took out his blue-lined notebook and his guitar and, eventually, they got to work. Tom didn't end up leaving till five in the morning. The first song the pair ever wrote together was called 'Chills in the Evening', which came together that first fateful night, but it wouldn't be the last. Tom spoke openly about their partnership in *Unsaid Things*:

I think we both knew that we'd stumbled upon something pretty special . . . Despite [my] looking up to Matt Willis in a big way ever since I'd been at school, I think I realised that I had more in common with James. As time passed, I grew to realise that in James I had found an amazing friend and mentor. He taught me everything I know about songwriting, and I truly believe that he is one of the most underrated talents of our time – a genius with an amazingly contagious creative energy.

But the 'genius' was running into a problem. Busted's debut album, *Busted*, was released just after the whirlwind of their first single, on 30 September 2002. It staggered drunkenly into the charts at number 30 – much like Matt after one of his special 'cocktails' as some unkindly joked – and then slumped into the hundreds, a dead weight around number 141, and seemingly dead to the world, too.

Were Busted just a one-off, one-hit wonder?

THREE

Not Alone

Busted's management and the record label tried to put their minds at rest. It was highly unusual to release a full album so close to the debut single; they were confident sales would pick up in due course. They were playing the long game. For the band at least, though, it was a nail-biting time. The second single wasn't due out until the new year, so for now all they could do was throw themselves into the promotion, which included playing loads of live gigs, including a slot on the autumn *Smash Hits* 2002 tour.

For James, as ever, it was all about the music. Having found his songwriting soulmate in Tom, he was flying as fast as a DeLorean car at 88 m.p.h. – and he wasn't about to slow down. Most nights, no matter what gig James had been at, no matter what the hour, Tom was invited round to Princess Park Manor to write. James recalled of that time, in a solo interview with The Vault, 'I would get our manager to get him round in a car. And after I would get home he would come round and we'd write late at night till about three or four, sometimes five in the morning. We would write a song a night. It was a cool time.'

So cool, in fact, that Tom quit college; he was, you might say, too cool for school. By night, he would write songs with James; by day, well, Rashman and Fletch had another proposition for him, one they hoped might connect him with his longed-for band-mates. With the record company feeling confident about Busted's success – the top-three hit single was in the bag, and the album sales were slowly, slowly on the rise – they asked Prestige Management if it would be interested in putting together a more manufactured band for them, in the vein of a traditional boy band. Prestige was keen to pursue the opportunity – and asked Tom if he wanted to be in the group. But Tom, at the age of seventeen, had learned a thing or two about himself as an artist by now, and knew the set-up wouldn't suit him. He wanted to play his own instruments, write his own songs and have his own band.

However, he was up for coming along for the audition ride. He was paid to sort the hopefuls' application forms and film the performances: every glossy, flicky-haired, beautifully polished last one of them.

The advert for the new band, which would eventually become known as V, specified that the management were looking for 'pop singers, not rock singers, so please do not bring guitars'. Little wonder, then, that the auditionees – and there were lots of them – were of the preppy, clean-cut variety, eager to show off their dance moves and their teenage-heartthrob dulcet tones. City after city, Tom patiently worked his camcorder and dreamed of the kind of bandmate he wanted for his group. Someone who could play an instrument brilliantly, he thought. Someone cool. Someone with a bit of an edge; a cockiness to counterbalance Tom's natural reticence. There was a lot of confidence on display at the V auditions, but none of the hopefuls was even halfway right for Tom's vision for his band.

Then came Manchester. The boy stood out because he had a guitar, blatantly ignoring the instructions in the ad. He also had shaggy dark hair, a thick Northern accent – and heaps of star quality.

'All right,' he said, as he stood across from Fletch and Rashman in the crowded audition room, with Tom peering out at him from behind his camcorder in the corner. 'My name's Danny Jones.'

Danny Jones was from Bolton and proud of it. On the cusp of his seventeenth birthday, he was a huge fan of Oasis and his absolute idol Bruce Springsteen, of Ocean Colour Scene and Pink Floyd. The Backstreet Boys certainly weren't a part of his musical vocabulary.

> **He had shaggy dark hair, a thick Northern accent – and heaps of star quality**

He'd first picked up a guitar as a very, very small toddler; he'd had a plastic toy model that he'd cherished as most other kids would a cuddly bear. Aged six, he got his first 'proper' guitar from Argos and started formal lessons – he would eventually go on to pass his Grade 6 with honours – before upgrading to an Encore guitar when he was twelve. It was two years later, when he was fourteen, that he gave a performance that changed his life. There was a talent contest happening at a local working men's club, and his mum, Kath, encouraged him to enter, even though he wasn't sure he could sing. Aside from a one-off performance in a school production of *Bugsy Malone*, albeit as the lead, he'd tended to concentrate on his instrumental skills, playing lead guitar in other school shows such as *Grease* and *Jesus Christ Superstar*.

With his mum's encouragement ringing in his ears, he found himself taking to the stage. He belted out the Gallagher brothers' 'Don't Look Back in Anger', just as Matt Willis had done before him in another pub down South, a year or so earlier. Danny won second place. It wasn't his greatest performance, but it gave him a bit of self-belief; and that was worth its weight in gold. He went on to form his own band, Jinx, and they were winning talent contests before too long.

It was good to have something going right, because Danny's home life wouldn't be taking first prize in any kind of contest. For as long as he could remember, his mum and dad hadn't seen eye to eye. They were different people, with different interests, and his dad did a tough job: he was a prison warder, which made him a tough man. That could sometimes come in useful on the rough streets of Bolton, especially when Danny was being chased by kids from a rival postcode area, but it didn't make him an easy man to live with. Some of Danny's earliest memories were of his parents arguing as he lay awake in bed, listening to them fight. He and his sister Vicky would lose themselves in music as they grew up; she was an accomplished singer and he would often accompany her on his guitar as she sang in the pubs and clubs around Bolton.

It was Vicky who had spotted the ad for the new band. She'd printed it out for Danny to have a look at, but their printer – unreliable at the best of times – had somehow missed out the word 'not' in the advert. So, when Danny rocked up to the audition, guitar firmly in hand and a Stereophonics song lined up as his show-stopping piece, he was fully expecting the management to be looking for rock singers who could play the guitar like Springsteen. As he surveyed the acrobatic warm-ups of his fellow auditionees, he felt that he was in the wrong place at the wrong time. But there was no flying time machine to get him out of this one.

His mum urged him to go ahead with the audition anyway. It was, after all, a major management company and a major record label pulling the strings of this particular puppet boy band. 'You don't know what you might get out of it.'

So Danny did his thing, performing the Verve's 'Bittersweet Symphony' in the end – the closest he could come to pop at such short notice. He was talented enough to get through to the next round, but, to be taken seriously at this boy-band audition, he was going to have to sing a straight-up pop song. The only trouble was, he didn't know any.

He felt like he was in the wrong place at the wrong time

That was where Tom came in: at the panel's request, he agreed to teach Danny a Backstreet Boys song for his next audition for the new group. He and Tom took their guitars and holed up in the corridor outside the main audition room, laboriously picking out each note of 'I Want It That Way' until Danny had it down pat. His sister Vicky helped, and before long Danny had nailed it. As he recalled in *Unsaid Things*, 'To my surprise, I really liked it. I'd never heard straight, clean pop chords like that, and I found them so satisfying to play.'

As for the panel, they were finding Danny himself mighty satisfying, too. He was down to the last fifteen for V, but Rashman, Fletch and Tom were all wondering if he might be better suited to Tom's vision for his band. Yet that would mean asking Danny to give up a place in a record-label-backed, management-guaranteed band for a chance on making it with an unsigned teenager who wrote songs in his bedroom. Would he really go for it?

Rashman got to know him a little better to find out. Following that first V audition, he invited Danny to London. They met in the business lounge of the InterContinental and Danny sipped a Diet Coke as Rashman grilled him on his hopes and ambitions for the future, and chatted more to him about his songwriting; Danny had showcased a couple of original tracks in Manchester, and Rashman had been impressed. Like most sixteen-year-olds, Danny didn't really have much of an idea as to what he really wanted to do, but one thing was certain: he wanted to play guitar. The one thing V probably wouldn't allow him to do.

On 27 October 2002, not long after the first V auditions, Tom and Rashman were in Manchester again, this time to support Busted, who were performing their slot on the *Smash Hits* tour at the Manchester Arena. Casually, Tom invited Danny to come along. The gig pretty much blew Danny's mind: great songs, great stagecraft, great guitar riffs, great girls hollering their heads off in the audience ... *This* was what he wanted to be doing. When Tom told him he was mates with Busted, he was seriously awestruck.

But before too long he was mixing with them, too. A few weeks later, the final-stage auditions for V took place in London, with Tom filming them as usual, and James was hanging out with his new writing pal. Tom and Danny ended up sharing a hotel room, and, when James kipped over too, the writing duo topped and tailed in the same bed. Not that there was much sleeping going on. How could there be, when there was so much music to be played?

Tom and James were bowled over by Danny's guitar-playing abilities. His Grade 6 technique, backed up by a natural show-manship and a lifelong love of rock, had resulted in some seriously jaw-dropping skills. And the respect went both ways, as Danny recalled in *Unsaid Things*:

We would stay up all night in that hotel, listening to music, messing around, playing guitar . . . As we played together, there was an instant connection. Tom and I both seemed to know what the other person was going to do. And then, out of the blue, he'd start singing harmonies to my vocal lines. Harmonies? I was amazed – I didn't know how he did it, but I knew we had something special.

They could all sense it: Tom, Danny – and James. The connec-tion wasn't just musical: the three of them enjoyed a laugh together, too. It was so obvious that, when the time came for Danny to make a call about his future, he didn't hesitate. He turned down the opportunity to be in V, and returned to Bolton with a plan to somehow work with Tom. He headed back up North without a record deal and without any firm plans in place –

but, this time, as he later wrote in a song, he was 'not alone'. He'd found his musical mates.

From that moment on, they would often send tapes back and forth of songs they were writing and ideas they'd had, and Danny would come and stay with Tom at his parents' house as often as he could. It was like Matt and James all over again, jamming in James's parents' house in Southend – except that, on this occasion, one member of the triumvirate just happened to be in what was fast becoming Britain's biggest band.

Just as the record label had said, the *Busted* album had been a slow burner, and, as Christmas passed and 2002 turned into 2003, it caught fire in a raging golden blaze. Indeed, a gold record, marking a staggering 100,000 copies sold, was presented to James, Matt and Charlie on *Top of the Pops Saturday* on 20 January 2003, the same day they released their second single: James's much-loved 'Year 3000'.

The choice for the follow-up hadn't been as straightforward as selecting 'What I Go to School For'. Charlie's vote was for something like 'Without You', a moody, dark ballad that showcased their more serious side, while James was always keen on the time-travel track – not least because he wanted to see whether the video might be able to emulate the classic *Back to the Future*. He recalled writing the track in *Busted*; it was one of the songs from their Southend days:

We'd just been messing around with lyrics – singing a line, then singing another line, and somehow we got on to time travel. Some songwriters I really admire will be writing songs to a really strict brief from their record labels, or their management, but we were just trying everything out. All of our really good songs have come really quickly – almost out of nowhere.

'Year 3000' definitely wasn't a record-company-brief kind of song. So authentically James Bourne it could be his personal theme tune, the imaginative track not only name-checks his idol Michael Jackson and elements from his favourite film, *Back to the Future*, but also references naked three-

Nude triple-breasted ladies were really *not* on the wishlist

breasted women (another classic-cinema nod, this time to 1990's Mars-based movie *Total Recall*). Nude triple-breasted ladies were really *not* what a commercially minded management targeting the teen market would have put on the wishlist!

Yet, for the innovative and wild-child Busted, it was the perfect second single – and the fans clearly agreed. Boosted by a cartoon-tastic video, which featured James's little brother Chris as the infamous neighbour Peter, the record sold in its thousands. It went straight in at number two and was still in the top ten three months later.

If you hadn't heard of them before, you would now: 'Year 3000' was undoubtedly the song that put Busted on the map. And, with their album being described by *Q* as 'inspired' and by the *NME* as 'the best album about being a teenager in recent memory', they were on top of the world. The album's artwork – the three lads standing in front of an iconic height chart, as if they were in a police line-up; the entire image stamped with the red Busted logo – was dominating the shelves of record shops across the globe. For James, who had recently been reunited with his school sweetheart Kara, life couldn't get much better.

Those around them were keen to counsel the young stars on the hurricane of fame that was about to sweep them away. In *Busted*, Matt recalled that Uri Geller – Michael Jackson's good friend, much to James's excitement – had taken them aside when they'd appeared on *The Saturday Show* to impart some pearls of wisdom. Matt said, 'Uri's advice was basically, "Have a brilliant time, make the very most of everything, but don't get into drugs. You get into the industry and it's paved with drugs. Stay your own man."'

Matt was by now merrily enjoying a daily spliff in the way most people have a morning coffee

It was good advice, but for Matt, who was by now merrily enjoying a daily spliff in the way most people have a morning coffee, it came a little too late. Cannabis aside, however, he wasn't a druggie in the traditional sense. Alcohol was his drug of choice, and, with so much to celebrate, every night was party night in Mattie Jay's world.

It was a world that James didn't live in, as Tom recalled in *Unsaid Things*,

James was a lot like me: a bit geeky, he didn't drink and he didn't smoke. His bandmates Charlie and Matt weren't quite so clean-living. With a Busted theatre tour coming up, James knew his bandmates would be partying harder than him, so he asked me if I'd like to come on tour with them so that he and I could start writing Busted's second album together.

The tour wasn't due to start until May, but Tom said yes straightaway. Even before the tour began, he and James were coming up with new songs. As a private joke between the two of them, they compared the art of hit-making to fishing, and they soon found that the tunes were flowing with the boys reeling in hit after hit. On Tuesday, 4 March 2003, Tom headed round to James's flat as usual. The apartment was quiet: Charlie had moved out the month before, seeking a bit more independence.

It was Shrove Tuesday, so at first James and Tom joked that they should pen a ditty in honour of Pancake Day; as Tom later recalled on *Fearne and McBusted*. But that idea didn't get much further than a song title at the top of the page in Tom's notebook, which was filled with doodles as well as lyrics. They turned their attention to another track instead, and that proved to be much more productive. By the end of the night, they'd completed a crazy little tune that they called 'Crashed the Wedding'. It featured, as was beginning to be a theme, a reference to a movie: 1993's *Wayne's World 2*, as the hapless hero of the song crashes a wedding being held on the film's Gordon Street.

Matt loved the track as soon as he heard it, especially the line that riffed on a vicar's opening speech to a wedding congregation: 'We are gathered here today . . .'; he dubbed it 'genius' to Culturewatch. The song also linked perfectly to a track on Busted's debut album, with the hero dubbing himself a 'Loser Kid', the name of the closing song on *Busted*. The budding songwriting team of Bourne–Fletcher thought they had a hit on their hands, but only time would tell.

Hits were what Busted were racking up at an astonishing rate. Just under a month before the theatre tour kicked off, on 21 April, they released their third single from their debut album, which was the song they'd written about Charlie's knockback from Daisy Bell, 'Crash and Burn'. Due to the *Columbia* space shuttle disaster, which had occurred on 1 February, the track was renamed 'You Said No' in sensitivity to the families of the seven deceased astronauts.

Matt, James and Charlie were a little apprehensive about where the song might place, because by this point, with the album having gone gold, lots of fans already had the song in their collections. Would it sell?

They needn't have worried. As the chart rundown began on Sunday, 27 April, the boys kept waiting and waiting to hear their track. Radio 1 presenter Wes Butters kept them hanging on till the bitter end. Just before 7 p.m., 'You Said No' was played to the nation as the UK's number one. Busted were at the top of the charts for the very first time. And they couldn't be happier.

'Slap my bum, we're number one!' Matt cried with typical exuberance, before donning some 'celebratory eyeliner' for their performances on *CD:UK* and *Top of the Pops*.

And there was a lot to celebrate: Busted were the first ever band whose first three singles had charted in such a steady yet meteoric rise to chart domination, hitting numbers three, two and one respectively. Their achievement was officially entered into *Guinness World Records*.

After just shy of eighteen months together, Busted had made music history. And they were determined that their first headlining tour would be one to remember, too. By now, the lads had put in a lot of time on the road, whether on the *Smash Hits* UK tour or travelling to meet their international fans in Germany, Sweden and other countries. They'd become accustomed to the long hours – and had found their own ways of filling the time and entertaining themselves. For Matt, that usually involved some kind of trouble, as he revealed in *Busted*: 'We've actually managed to get ourselves banned from one chain of hotels. We accidentally got really, really pissed one night and ran riot through the entire place, and as a consequence we're not allowed to stay there again.'

James remembered seeing Matt hanging out of the window of his fifth-floor bedroom, balanced precariously on the window ledge, on one particular night, while Matt's friend Lee Ryan would sometimes join them for wild nights out both home and abroad. James recalled in *Busted*, 'One time we met up with him in Munich and got so hammered on B52s, White Russian cocktails, tequilas, beers … We've got video footage of one point in the evening and we just look as if

> **James remembered seeing Matt hanging out the window of his fifth-floor bedroom**

we're about to die.' That night ended with Charlie vomiting all over his hotel room (including inside Matt's suitcase); Matt losing his shoes and socks – meaning he had to travel to the airport the next day with bare feet; and all three of them missing their flight home, at a cost of some eight grand to the record label. But, despite their high and somewhat alcoholic spirits, they were all professionals at heart and the partying never got too out of hand; as *HR* magazine put it, their manager's role had 'yet to include explaining to a hotel manager why there's a television-shaped hole in the hotel room's window and a Rolls-Royce in the swimming pool'.

What the band were really psyched about was performing live. All three of them adored that incomparable buzz of standing onstage and singing your heart out; it was why they were in a band in the first place. The sold-out tour ahead of them, which was due to take in sizeable venues such as the Hammersmith Apollo in London, would see whole theatres of fans singing their songs back to them. This was the big time, and for Matt the theatre tour was 'the best thing that had ever happened in my life', as he later told The Vault.

And Tom Fletcher, with Danny just a phone call away, was with them all the way. As May drew to a close, Tom and the three Busted boys packed their bags, zipped their guitars into their carry-cases, and stepped on board the tour bus for the ride of their young lives.

The tour opened on 17 May in Newport and lasted for the next month, taking in Nottingham, Newcastle, Sheffield, Glasgow, Manchester and other towns and cities. The reaction from fans was indescribable – and not just to Matt's bleached blond hair. As Tom put it in *Unsaid Things*, 'There was mayhem everywhere they went.'

There was mayhem everywhere they went

While Matt enjoyed the party lifestyle, and other attractions (by his own admission to the *Mirror*, he 'made the most of being a young man in a band when it came to women'), James and Tom embraced not the girls, but the opportunity to write. They were inspired by the mad world around them and their blossoming partnership. Night after night, they would write song after song. And, with Tom and Danny having decided they were going to form a band, they weren't just writing for Busted any more. Tom had ambitions to play his own music in his own band. So he and James channelled their creativity not only into tunes for Busted's much-anticipated second album, which the label wanted to release later that year, but also songs for Tom and Danny's new, and as yet nameless, group. Each night after the show, Tom and James would retire to James's hotel room, order nothing more rock 'n' roll than milkshakes to see them through the night, and then write until the sun came up.

Matt and Charlie were usually out partying, but one evening Charlie joined the duo and they came up with a tune called 'That Thing You Do'. It was different from most of Busted's other songs. While the guitars were still there, and the cheeky lyrics, it had a summery lightness to it that was new. It was more of a sixties-style surf record than a Blink-182-inspired track. And it was a hugely important development, as Tom remembered in *Unsaid Things*: 'For the first time, we'd come up with something that was fresh and original that would be more suited to whatever *my* project was going to be ... That song was the spark for everything that was to come.'

With the new direction nailed, Tom and James became more productive than ever. Jotted down in Tom's black book, '5 Colours in Her Hair' followed 'Air Hostess'; there followed yet another song – and another. In less than two weeks, they had a raft of tunes that they were proud of – but still no name for the new group.

Rashman tried to help them out, suggesting Skate Park as a name; perhaps inspired by Busted's 'You Said No' video, which saw stunts on a half-pipe interspersed with footage of the band playing live (and Matt crowd surfing). Tom and Danny weren't keen, but they weren't having any luck themselves in coming up with something better.

On Wednesday, 21 May, the Busted tour bus pulled into Sheffield to rig their gig at City Hall. Tom – yawning from yet another late night writing with James – sat in the empty theatre seats as the band ran through their sound check. Idly, his brain started turning over the problem of the band name. It couldn't be anything too fake. It couldn't be anything too cheesy. It had some-how to be authentic, but he was stumped if he had a clue what.

Onstage, Busted moved seamlessly from one track into the next, Matt's bass guitar picking out the opening notes of 'Year 3000'. Tom smiled: he loved this song; and his and James's shared love of eighties movies and *Back to the Future* was a big part of their friendship. Only James could get 'flux capacitor' into the lyric of a song. James – and maybe Marty McFly . . .

Though they weren't yet testing the pyrotechnics onstage, a veritable firework went off in Tom's head. McFly. McFly! It was perfect. Cool, catchy and totally genuine. He raced backstage – the sound check over – and grabbed James to tell him the good news, as he remembered in *Unsaid Things*:

James stared at me. His eyes widened. And then he went absolutely nuts. 'That's so cool, that's so cool! Quick, tell Danny . . .'

I told Danny the good news. 'McFly!'

Silence.

Mr Jones was going to need some convincing.

FOUR

Room on the 3rd Floor

I f there was one thing Tom and James were passionate about, it was *Back to the Future* (music aside). Danny's unfamiliarity with the classic Robert Zemeckis movie was like a red rag to two very enraged bulls. They had to make Danny see what a totally awesome, supercool idea it was to name the new band McFly. As soon as Busted were back from the tour, Danny was in for a night to remember.

The Busted tour finished on 3 June 2003. Not long after, Danny found himself knocking on the door of James's swish London flat at Princess Park Manor and being escorted into the sitting room like a guest of honour. The black-leather, bachelor-pad La-Z-Boys were already set up in front of the enormous TV, with Danny getting the prime position with a perfect view of the set. Tom and James presented him with multilayered sandwiches and the best milkshakes known to man (they were true experts after their excessive consumption via hotel room service on the Busted tour). Danny, milkshake in one hand and a good dose of scepticism about the proposed band name in the other, lay back in the chair and prepared to be impressed.

Tom and James kept casting sly looks at him as he watched the film, exchanging meaningful glances with each other if he laughed at the funny bits or exclaimed at the cool ones. A car chase! Skateboarding to 'The Power of Love'! The flux capacitor! A soaring theme tune that totally kicked ass! It was the best film ever.

They'd been watching for a little over an hour. On the screen, Marty McFly had got himself in deep trouble by standing up to bully Biff Tannen at the diner. He'd legged it, nicked a kid's toy to make a makeshift skateboard, and was currently being chased by Biff and his gang in Biff's very smart black Ford motor car. Marty was winning, sending sparks flying from the tail of his board, when Biff's convertible suddenly had him cornered and was ramming him straight towards a manure truck. McFly, spotting the danger, courageously leaped on to the bonnet of the car, clambered over the cronies and jumped back onto his skateboard, just in time to see Biff and the convertible crash into the truck and get covered in horse manure.

It was an exciting scene by anyone's standards – but that wasn't what had snagged Danny's attention. Sitting up straight in his La-Z-Boy, his mind whirling, barely able to believe his eyes, he ordered Tom and James to rewind the movie.

They did. They paused it on his direction. Writ large on the screen, in big white capital letters painted onto the side of the wooden manure truck, was a name.

D. Jones.

There could be only two reactions to a coincidence like that. The first was to exclaim 'Great Scott!' like Doc Emmett Brown. The second was to agree 100 per cent that the new band's name *had* to be McFly.

From there, they were on a roll. Amid great excitement, James and Tom got out their guitars and enthusiastically played Danny 'That Thing You Do'. Like them, he completely dug the vibe of the track, and the three of them were soon tinkering about with a new song; the first they'd all written together from scratch as a threesome.

As always, they cast about for their theme by chatting about their own lives. For Tom, his inspiration, as it so often was, was fixated on Giovanna, his ex-girlfriend from school. Unlike James and his childhood sweetheart Kara Tointon, who were back together despite their earlier split, Tom and Giovanna were still separated – and Gi was even dating someone new: an older guy who worked in the police force. Needless to say, Tom hated his guts.

As only good friends can, James and Danny immediately saw the humour of Tom's predicament, and teased him mercilessly if good-naturedly. But the scenario wasn't just the source of a good joke at a friend's expense: it was also the source of a new song. 'Obviously' was the result, and it sparked a summer of stunning songs.

As only good friends can, James and Danny immediately saw the humour of Tom's predicament, and teased him mercilessly

Tom and Danny would split their time between Tom's parents' house, Room 363 at the InterContinental (inspiration for their tune 'Room on the Third Floor'), and James's place at Princess Park Manor. While the three of them were writing at the Busted house one week, they came up with a plethora of songs that they thought could do something: 'Surfer Babe', 'She Left Me', 'Broccoli', 'That Girl' and 'Down by the Lake'. McFly's debut album was coming together at super-speed.

Yet James was also concentrating on the other album in his life: Busted's second, which would be called *A Present for Everyone*. He and Tom had produced several songs for the record written just by the two of them – 'Crashed the Wedding', 'Who's David?', 'Over Now' and 'Loner in Love' – but Busted's other members were also accomplished songwriters and they had a lot of creativity to contribute too, both with and without Tom. Charlie and Matt both wrote their own songs for the album, Matt collaborating with Robbie Williams's famous co-writer Guy Chambers and producer Steve Power to produce the rocky tracks 'Fake' and 'Better Than This'.

A trip to LA to record with the hit producers the Matrix, who had just produced Avril Lavigne's album *Let Go* – the biggest pop/rock debut of 2002 – was also on the cards. It resulted in some dramatic tracks co-written by the band and the producers, including '3am' and 'She Wants to Be Me'. The latter was a clever song riffing on the boys' assessment of the attentions of some of their 'fans'. Much as Matt might have been enjoying their – ahem – affection, even he could see that, sometimes, the fame was what the girls were after more than the man.

For Matt, he knew what he wanted in a woman, but as yet he

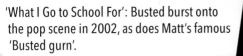
'What I Go to School For': Busted burst onto the pop scene in 2002, as does Matt's famous 'Busted gurn'.

Busted: the final line-up. From top to bottom: Charlie Simpson, Matt Willis, James Bourne. Auditionee Tom Fletcher is nowhere to be seen.

Jumping for joy: Busted storm to the top of the charts and make the *Guinness World Records* with their first three singles.

Not one but two BRIT Awards: Busted claim Best Pop and Best British Breakthrough at the BRITs 2004.

Where it all began: both Busted and McFly spent a lot of their early days at the InterContinental in London, forever immortalised in the song 'Room on the Third Floor'.

The luxurious Princess Park Manor in north London, home to Busted and McFly and scene of some totally awesome songwriting.

And then there were two: Tom Fletcher and Danny Jones decide to start their own band.

Magic McFly: the full line-up sees the band make history in 2004 as the youngest group ever to have a debut number-one album.

All about you: after the shock Busted split, McFly rule the world, collecting Best Pop at the BRITs 2005. From left to right: Danny Jones, Dougie Poynter, Tom Fletcher, Harry Judd.

hadn't found it. Writing in *Busted*, he said, 'I like girls who are intelligent, with their head screwed on, who can tell me when I'm letting myself down but do so without nagging me.' For now, the search continued – and he certainly had plenty of opportunity to try out candidates for the role of girlfriend.

As for Tom and Danny, they were trying out candidates for a bassist and a drummer to join their crew. That summer writing with James, they laid down some early demos of 'Obviously' and 'Surfer Babe', and started advertising for bandmates in the *Stage* and other places. But barely anyone turned up to their low-key auditions – certainly no one suitable. Their hearts sank. But their songs were about to get them a golden ticket to the big time.

Fletch and Rashman had been overseeing the evolution of the new band and, with the demo now in the bag, thought the time was right to start showcasing Tom and Danny to record labels. The two of them were soon scheduled to meet the biggest record execs in the country to play acoustic sets of their songs. They were both just seventeen, and they'd been writing songs together for perhaps nine months at most. They were scared, to say the least. James and Matt gave them loads of encouragement, remembering how they'd felt when it had been them touring the record companies, eighteen months before.

The pep talk paid off: when Tom and Danny were offered a record deal with the same label as Busted, Island Records, the four of them became label-mates as well as very good friends. Yet, with a record deal now in place, Tom and Danny *really* needed to find some fellow musicians to make up the band – and fast.

Enter Harry Judd. With a record label and Busted's manage-ment now attached to the auditions, they were suddenly a much hotter bet than Tom and Danny's more amateur attempts to find a crew. And word soon got around about the tryouts, especially at Uppingham, Charlie Simpson's alma mater and Harry's current

Enter Harry Judd

school, where, as the summer term drew to a close, the boys were keen to follow in their former classmate's footsteps. Harry was a school year younger than Charlie and didn't know him well, but the school was a small one, with fewer than 800 pupils in the entire student body, and he'd heard gossip on the Uppingham grapevine that other boys were planning to attend. Why not him too?

It was an ambitious move. He'd been playing the drums for only eighteen months, but Harry was an ambitious boy – and a dedicated and talented one, too. When he put his mind to something, he *really* put his mind to it, and usually, given a bit of time, he would excel.

He'd come to music in a roundabout way. Childhood lessons on the guitar and trumpet had left him unfulfilled. It was his natural outgoing friendly nature that led to a change. His mates – like most of the school – were in a band, a three-piece called Boy Genius, and, when their drummer left, Harry had the wizard idea that he could take his place and have fun jamming with his friends. He got a second-hand drum kit and a laid-back teacher to tutor him in the rhythms of the Red Hot Chili Peppers and Rage Against the Machine, and he was away. He used to nick the key to the rehearsal room so he could practise at any given moment, and, from that point on, his drumsticks were never far from his hands.

He had them tucked into his back pocket as he waited in line outside the Covent Garden studio for his turn to audition. He didn't necessarily know it, but Tom and Danny knew he was coming. The Uppingham old boys had put a word in via Charlie, so they knew exactly who he was as he strode confidently into the audition room, trying to give the impression that he was clearly the rock god they'd been looking for, while inside feeling just as scared as everyone else . . .

There was another auditionee there that morning who was definitely scared. Petrified, in fact. He'd already thrown up once with nerves, and the acid at the back of his throat was threatening to make it an encore. His name was Dougie Poynter.

Dougie was an anxious child. Nervous, jumpy. One of the most unpopular kids in the school. In the small town of Corringham, Essex, where he came from, people weren't big on seeing beyond first impressions to the lovely person inside. Dougie was a skater boy, into boarding and rock music; he bred lizards as a hobby; he was shy and awkward; and he was diminutive for his age. He was a walking target.

The one place he felt at home was behind his guitar. Discovering Blink-182, as for James and Matt and Tom before him, had been an epiphany. Like Danny, he'd started to learn guitar on a cheap instrument from Argos, when he was thirteen; he then switched to the bass when a mate, who also played guitar, convinced him that mastering the bass would be simpler because it had only four strings. Plus, they could then form a band. Ataiz was the result, and they'd not been going long when Dougie heard about the McFly audition at Gable Hall Performing Arts School, where he spent most of his time mooching through the corridors, trying not to get spat on or beaten up.

There was only one problem: the ad said it was looking for musicians over the age of sixteen. Dougie was born in November 1987, so, in that summer of 2003, he was still only fifteen. He decided not to let it bother him and asked his mum to take him along to the audition. He knew he'd need her cheerleading him on to get him through the door – and he was right. Standing there in his skater clothes, staring bug-eyed at the hundreds of other boys, who all seemed so much more confident than he was, he felt like one of his lizards: his blood ran cold.

In fact, the skater clothes made him stand out straightaway to Tom and Danny, Fletch and Rashman. Dougie may have been unpopular at school, but the difference that got him noticed there got him noticed here for all the *right* reasons. With his spiked fair hair and his casual look, he was just what they wanted. They had their eye on him, and on Harry – who had bleached his usually brown hair blond and was wearing a band T-shirt – from the start.

Dougie felt like one of his lizards: his blood ran cold

But looks weren't everything: the musicianship was key. Dougie was up first. He'd been planning on playing something from his first love, Blink-182, but Fletch floored him by asking for some pop. Dougie's mind cast about frantically for something he could play, and then he gratefully recalled that he'd just about managed to pick up 'Billie Jean' when he was messing about in his bedroom a couple of days earlier. That would have to do. He took a deep breath, and started playing.

Sitting across from him in the audition room, Tom sat up just that little bit straighter. Michael Jackson? Oh, yes please: this guy *rocked*! He looked the part, he was playing Tom's favourite idol. Surely he was in the band?

The intro to 'Billie Jean' is quite a famous one: those first eight notes repeated, and then the thumping bass line that gets dance floors pumping the world over. Dougie played the first eight notes. *OK, this is good, this is going well.* He played them again. And then he hit a brick wall. It was only once he'd started playing the song that he realised he didn't know the rest. His attention had wandered that other day in his bedroom, and he'd never, well, finished it. He'd never got to the end, or learned how to play the whole song. And now he was stuck, standing like a lemon in front of a panel of highly important people, playing the same eight notes over and over. And over again.

One more time.

And another.

Once more with feeling.

And, er, one more time again.

It was Tom who brought his ordeal to an end. 'OK, dude, that's enough.' Dougie's heart sank. He tried to win them round by playing them a song he'd written, 'The Last Girl Story', but, no matter how good a songwriter he was, the 'Billie Jean' audition had been utterly criminal, not at all smooth. Dougie recalled how awful he felt in *Unsaid Things*: 'I was in that room for about half an hour with just one thought in my head: I'd totally blown it. When I get nervous my whole body feels uncomfortable. I just want to unzip myself and jump out. I had that feeling then.'

Harry, meanwhile, was – with his usual panache – impressing the panel, demonstrating his drum solos and even trying to sing a bit. Together with Danny, he sat in front of the camera and warbled his way through Busted's 'Year 3000'. When the cull of the first auditions came, Harry and Dougie were asked to remain, much to Dougie's surprise. But Tom and Danny had liked him. Perhaps he was just paralysed with nerves, they'd reasoned. He was given the benefit of the doubt – but he was going to have to up his game.

It was weird for Tom and Danny, being on the other side of the audition. They could feel the hopefuls' eyes on them whenever they popped their heads out to call the next person in, or even just walked through the corridor to go and get a drink. To the auditionees, these were the guys who were already in the band. They were cool. They had it. 'They' hadn't known exactly how to dress that morning – Danny was in his usual ripped dark jeans and a casual T-shirt, while Tom wore a striped shirt and loose trousers – but they could have worn a spacesuit and the candidates would have thought them the epitome of funk. If Tom had had time to think of it, he might have cast his mind back to his Busted audition, when Matt was already in the band and he'd looked up to him with such wide eyes; but, with their tight schedule, there wasn't a second to think of anything but the difficult task at hand.

In the afternoon, Tom and Danny were on display once again, when Fletch asked for their demo to be played to the whittled-down aspirants. The speakers blared with the strains of 'Surfer Babe' and 'Obviously'. Tom and Danny scanned the faces of the contenders as they sat in the audition room. Did they like it? Who was digging it? What did they *really* think? It was as though their hearts, rather than their songs, were being squeezed out through the amps.

Dougie, for one, was in seventh heaven. 'It was genius,' he remembered in *Unsaid Things*, 'like Green Day meets the Beach

Boys . . . I *had* to be in this band.' Danny got the remaining guys up on their feet and accompanied them on his beloved guitar as they all sang along. And then the hopefuls were dismissed, and Dougie and Harry went home to wait for another word from Rashman.

Harry heard first. He was down to the last two, and summoned to a last-chance-saloon final audition at the InterContinental hotel in London. Rashman, who thought there was something about this well-to-do, hard-working, confident young man, had sent him McFly's demo beforehand. Unlike the other candidate, Harry had the upper hand of a week's practice in Uppingham's rehearsal room, playing along with the tracks that James, Danny and Tom had written that same summer, and learning the beats inside out and backwards. He was well prepared when he sauntered into the grand lobby of the Park Lane hotel and prepared to give the audition of his life.

But Martin, his rival, was a superb drummer. For two days they battled it out on the drums, playing about with Tom and Danny in and out of the audition room, and wondering who was going to make it. It was clear that Martin had skills that were far superior to Harry's; he had, after all, only been playing the drums for a year and a bit. Who were Danny and Tom going to choose? Danny recalled the dilemma in *Unsaid Things*:

Confession time: I was Team Martin. I wasn't really the type to think ahead, and was just looking at it from the point of view of who was the better drummer, whereas Tom, quite rightly, was remembering that we were choosing somebody who we'd hopefully be in a band with for ever . . .

While they were making up their minds, Dougie was opening his email from Richard Rashman. It was short and to the point. He hadn't made it. He wasn't good enough. He wasn't in the band.

Little Dougie Poynter – who never fought back against bullies, who kept his head down and his mouth shut and did anything for an easy life – made a decision the following day (after crying his eyes out, of course): he wasn't going to take this one lying down. He was going to put everything into being a better bass player. He emailed Rashman back and told him that he'd booked himself nightly bass lessons, and weekly singing lessons too. He was determined to do better. Rashman's reply was quick and typically brief: 'Keep me updated.'

Dougie made a decision: he wasn't going to take this one lying down

And Rashman had an update for Harry. It was Fletch who made the call – with the good news. He'd made it. He was in McFly. Harry was over the moon; he couldn't wait to tell his parents. The Judds, who had given their son the absolute best in life, and paid the very expensive fees of Uppingham for the past four years, were somewhat dubious about his plan to leave school at the tender age of seventeen to join a rock band. They sat him down that night to talk about it. What about university? What about his future career?

But Harry was adamant. He had to follow his heart.

Which was what Charlie Simpson was longing to do too. He'd said earlier in the year that if he was ever feeling 'self-indulgent' about his music, wanting to write *his* kind of tracks – the ones that didn't necessarily fit Busted's character as a highly commer-cial pop-punk band, which owed more to Charlie's harder rock and indie roots – then he would just keep the songs to himself. But as the months passed, and Busted chalked up yet another top-three hit in August with 'Sleeping with the Light On' – the first song James and Matt ever co-wrote – he was beginning to realise that keeping his songs to himself was kind of lonely.

But he didn't know what to do about it.

Little Dougie Poynter was a boy on a very big mission. He'd been wowed by Danny's awesome guitar skills during his failed McFly audition. Inspired by Danny's talent, he knuckled down to his les-sons and started challenging himself to get really good at the bass.

It wasn't easy. So much for the simple option. Most days he felt like Luke Skywalker trying to learn how to use the Force in his beloved *Star Wars* (Dougie was another one for classic sci-fi films). Still, he persevered, playing along to the Beatles and the Beach Boys – especially the latter, given the surf vibe of the demo he'd heard at the audition.

After a few weeks of intense hard work, Rashman suggested he meet with Dougie again. Why didn't he come to the InterContinental next weekend and they could have a chat? Dougie was thrilled. He'd felt like a boy at the last audition; he was determined that, this time, he would prove himself a man.

Dougie didn't know it then, but he was about to have to grow up faster than even he had planned.

The night before the all-important meeting with Rashman, he arrived home to find a weird atmosphere settled around his family house in Corringham. It had oozed into the corners and was thick with tension and upset. His mum was in tears. The extended family were in the kitchen, trying to comfort her. Dougie entered the room in confusion, looking round at the faces of his relatives and trying to work out what was wrong.

There was a short note on the side. It was from his dad. Dougie scanned it. But the words didn't make any sense.

His dad had left them: Dougie, his mum and his little sister Jasmine. He wasn't coming back. It was a total shock. Unlike Danny, whose parents were still working things out in Bolton, Dougie had never heard his parents fight. There'd never been a row that he could recall. Yet now his dad was gone – and Dougie was suddenly the man of the house.

His dad was the one who brought the money into their home. With him no longer around, Dougie would have to grow up fast. They couldn't afford for him to study the bass any longer. All that was gone. He made a bit of money selling the lizards he bred, and now he would have to channel all his income into paying the bills. But Dougie didn't mind – anything for his mum. He squared his shoulders. He would give up his dream of being in a band. He would look after her.

He would give up his dream of being in a band

He still had the meeting scheduled the next day with Rashman. His mum, who was distraught, wasn't going to be able to take him. Dougie bravely said he wouldn't go. But his uncle, listening in, said he would accompany him. So it was his uncle who travelled with him into town on the Tube, and gave him a good-luck hug as they stood outside the imposing white hotel. Dougie, carrying his guitar and his bass with his skinny little arms, hoisted them onto his back and walked, on his own, up to Rashman's suite.

Rashman could see how much he had improved, even in that very short time. But Dougie was perhaps one of the least confident people he'd ever met. Rashman – as well as listening to his songs and giving him musical advice – got him to rehearse saying hello and making eye contact. And he played him Charlie and Tom's Busted audition tapes to inspire him. Dougie, watching the sixteen-year-old Tom belt out BBMak's 'Back Here', wondered if he would ever be as good as that.

At the end of the meeting, as Rashman had done for Harry before him, Dougie was given the McFly demo to take away. Perhaps he could have a practice, the American suggested, maybe come in for another audition with the band in a week or so's time.

And so Dougie found himself walking into the InterContinental one more time, for one last chance. As with Harry and Martin, it was a sudden-death elimination contest. Two bassists. Two days. One. On. One.

For Tom, Danny and Harry, it wasn't an easy choice. Danny and Harry shared a room with the monosyllabic Dougie, who wouldn't even tell them his horoscope sign when they asked (having lied about his age, Dougie wasn't sure which star sign linked to his fictitious birthday). Was this silent guy really someone they wanted to tour with, write with and play onstage with?

For Tom in the adjoining room with Dougie's rival, said rival was perhaps taking it too much the other way. He was so comfortable with Tom that, in the middle of the night, Tom woke up to find the guy masturbating in the bed next to him. In all the times he and James or he and Danny had shared hotel rooms, *that* had certainly never happened before.

But Rashman was firmly Team Dougie. He played the three existing band members a video of Dougie performing his Blink-182-style songs with Ataiz, and they were sold. Dougie was in the band.

His rival, in a case of sour grapes, 'informed' on Dougie for being underage. But it didn't matter; in fact, it made them like Dougie more. They'd made their decision: McFly was born.

Now the hard work really started.

Hard work was something Busted could tell them all about. Their feet had barely touched the ground since their debut single had launched almost a year before. Life was an insane combination of gigs, photoshoots, recording sessions, writing sessions, travelling to gigs, meet-and-greets with fans, meet-and-greets with producers and fellow songwriters, interviews, more interviews, and more interviews still. They did the rounds of every magazine and every radio and TV show, from Radio 1 to MTV, and everyone wanted to know everything about them, from their favourite foods to their favourite colour. It wasn't quite why Charlie had joined a band.

In July, the band had published their first ever official book, *Busted*. (They weren't as good at coming up with imaginative titles for their output as they were at writing songs.) The book was filled with facts about the band – and lots and lots of glossy photos for their fans. James and Matt threw themselves into the bespoke shoots with insane enthusiasm. Matt's famous 'Busted gurn' appeared on almost every page, and it was also a perfect opportunity to showcase his new hairstyle – all of them: blond with a black streak, black with a blond streak, pale spikes, flat and fair, roots and no roots; he altered his look almost as frequently as he smoked grass.

On the opening page, next to a fore-word from the boys, James joined him in a Busted gurn and crazy hand gestures, pointing at Matt over the top of his head, while Matt, in the middle of the trio, pointed at both Matt and Charlie with his arms in a straitjacket-style stance. Charlie

Charlie smouldered; he didn't gurn

leaned against the wall, his hands in his pockets, pulling a pose that the agency Models 1 would have paid him good money for. Charlie smouldered; he didn't gurn.

And he was smouldering about all these songs he had that were no good to Busted. As he later revealed to *Kerrang!*, 'I had all of this creativity pent up inside and I just needed to vent it some-where, and I was writing a lot of songs but I couldn't play them.

'Because I didn't have anyone to play them with.'

FIVE

We Are the Young

With a light bump, the plane touched down on the runway at London Heathrow. James, Tom and Danny stretched in their seats after the long-haul flight. They'd been on holiday together to Florida, USA, visiting Walt Disney World – a much-needed break after all the songwriting they'd completed that summer. They shared a cab back to north London – Tom and Danny, together with Harry and Dougie, now lived ten minutes round the corner from James and Matt in a plush five-bedroom house in Finchley.

And Dougie and Harry certainly had a warm welcome home for them. For Dougie, the incredible accommodation was like a Magic Kingdom all his very own, especially given the tense home life he'd left behind him in Corringham. While Tom and Danny had been away, he and Harry had dipped into McFly's £500,000 record deal to kit themselves out with top-of-the-range instruments. Harry, who'd only ever had a second-hand drum kit before, was in heaven. Fully kitted out, Harry and Dougie had been practising the tricky demo tracks day in and day out. On their return, Tom and Danny were impressed both by their new bandmates' commitment and their increasing musical prowess.

As summer slipped into autumn, McFly concentrated on getting really tight in the rehearsal room, in preparation for recording their debut album in December, while Busted put the finishing touches to their second album. As ever, though, there was still time for partying. And like Matt Willis before them, it turned out that some of the McFly boys had a taste for weed.

It was Harry who first raised the subject with Danny, who knew Tom well enough to know that they had to keep it from him. Tom was cleaner than clean when it came to drugs and he would *not* have dug the side project the boys were planning on lighting up.

As for fifteen-year-old Dougie, fresh from home and the sudden loss of his dad, he'd have followed his bandmates anywhere, as he recalled in *Fearne and McBusted*: 'They played a lot of different roles for me. They were best friends, older brothers and dads all at the same time. They taught me how to do a lot of things for the first time – not dodgy things, [but things] like shaving; and they helped me open my first bank account.' Dougie was totally up for joining Danny and Harry for a cheeky smoke. It was a 'leading astray' that worked both ways though. Dougie said of Harry to Fearne, 'We were quite bad for each other. Harry doesn't have a stop button.'

Nevertheless, once he found out what was going on, Tom did

try to press it. When he discovered that the others were smoking dope every night in the house, he first burst into tears – shocked and worried that his dream of a successful band was over before it had begun – and then laid down some ground rules. Yet the others, even though they knew Tom was right, couldn't stop themselves from bending those rules a little.

It was in this climate that Tom met up with his old friend James. He was expecting him to reassure him, to give him some advice as to how to sort it out. But James had only one message for Tom, as Fletcher recalled in *Unsaid Things*.

'You four,' James had said to him, leaning forward to ram his message home, 'you've got to stick together. You've got to be a team.'

Because at that moment, Busted were anything but.

Not long before, at a party one evening, Charlie had met a guitarist called Alex Westaway and a drummer named Omar Abidi. They'd hit it off and started jamming that same night, playing a Rage Against the Machine track. A few days later, they went to a gig, then back to Charlie's place to play together again. To Charlie's delight, as the night wore on and

You've got to stick together. You've got to be a team

the sun started coming up, they wrote a new song together, something much more in keeping with the style he loved, called 'Too Much Punch'.

Charlie was in his element. This was what he'd been longing for: an outlet for his other songs, collaborators who were into the kind of music he really wanted to play. Soon, he was getting another band together, bringing in a bassist called Dan Haigh to join the original trio. They called their new band Fightstar.

It wasn't long before James and Matt realised what was going on; though, as James later revealed on *Fearne and McBusted*, 'He never really told me he was doing it.' Charlie acknowledged their difficulties in *Busted on Tour: The Official Book*. 'It's a sensitive issue which is a bit like stepping on glass.'

It was Fletch and Rashman who now stepped into the fragile arena to try to sort out the problems that were becoming more and more apparent. Charlie recalled, 'I had two long chats with Richard and Fletch. What frustrated me wasn't that I didn't like Busted, or that I didn't want to be in Busted. It was the fact that I didn't feel like what I wanted to do with Fightstar was being taken seriously. I was like, "This is really important for me, and I need to be happy about it to make it work."'

With James's words ringing in his ears that night, Tom made his way back to the McFly house. He didn't want his band to break up over this. He didn't want to be the odd one out. He wanted to get them through this so that they could enjoy success just like Busted – albeit without the personal fallings-out. So he called his bandmates together when he got back home and, for the sake of harmony, he joined them for a joint.

The long chats with Fletch and Rashman had put Charlie's mind at rest. He would continue with Fightstar – and with Busted, too. And as Hallowe'en passed, marking two years since Tom had been kicked out of Busted, the band geared up to their biggest single release yet, the first from their hotly anticipated second album: 'Crashed the Wedding'.

The video was one of the most fun they'd ever done. All three of them dressed up as different people at a wedding, playing all the different characters. James took the opportunity to dress up as a Michael Jackson tribute artist, complete with single sparkly glove, as part of the wedding band that opened the video. Matt, meanwhile, had a ball as the blushing bride, donning a snow-white bridal gown and veil with his usual energetic enthusiasm. He even ended up kissing himself – as 'Busted Matt' – midway through the shoot. And when he skateboarded across the top table on a silver platter, demonstrating some ace boarding skills that he might just have picked up from Dougie, it was certainly a video to remember.

Not least because of a special guest star that James and Matt had roped into proceedings. Although Charlie was an accomplished drummer, he was in full-on rock guitar (and pretty waitress) mode here. Who on earth could they get to play the drummer in the wedding band? There was only one possible answer. Step forward Mr Harry Judd.

Yet that wasn't the only Busted–McFly collaboration for the 'Crashed the Wedding' release. The B-side of the single was pretty special, too. It was a 'Busted featuring McFly' version of the Foundations' 1968 hit 'Build Me Up Buttercup' – the perfect way to introduce McFly's new sixties-style sound, albeit with a very Busted twist. It was also the very first official recording of Tom, Harry, Danny, Dougie, Matt and James all playing together.

The perfect way to introduce McFly's new sixties-style sound

The energy zings off the record from the very first syncopated bass line played by Matt and Dougie, all the way through to the very last thrum of the guitars at the end. It showcased all the thrashing chords that fans had come to expect of Busted, but complete with the soaring harmonies that McFly would soon be wowing the world with. Most of all, it was fun. High-energy. Fast-paced. Cheeky and enjoyable from start to finish, whether the boys were pursing their lips to sing – in near-comedy high-pitched voices – the 'yooooou' of the backing vocals, 'hey-hey-hey'-ing in unison, or relishing the classic 'call-and-return' chorus, belting it out to each other across the studio. It's a song you can't help but shake your shoulders to; and the fans clearly agreed. The single of 'Crashed the Wedding', complete with historic B-side, shot straight to the top of the charts, giving the Bourne–Fletcher writing partnership their very first number one. For Tom, who hadn't released a single of his own at that stage, it was an incredible landmark, made all the sweeter by the fact that he and Giovanna reunited around that time – and this time, he hoped it would be for good.

There was more success to come. A week after 'Crashed the Wedding' hit record stores, Busted performed the classic one-two knockout punch by following up with their second album, *A Present for Everyone*, which went on sale on 17 November. In the first three weeks, it sold as many copies as the eponymous *Busted* had in its entire run, and would go on to be certified three-times platinum with sales of over a million in the UK alone. It attracted plenty of positive reviews, too, with the BBC complimenting its 'irresistible pop songs with air-guitar riffs' and 'the sheer energy and enthusiasm that comes through in the music'. Meanwhile,

AbsolutePunk.net said, 'Rarely has music ever been or sounded so fun,' and the *Guardian* described it as 'fizzily effective'. In October, the *Observer Music Monthly* had proclaimed Busted as the heirs apparent of Britpop. This was their coronation.

Despite the jaw-dropping sales, it reached only number two in the charts – but James had no complaints about who had bested them. Their names were next to none other than Michael Jackson, whose *Number Ones* album was released that same week and took the top spot. In James's wildest dreams, he'd never have thought that his band would be up there with Jackson.

In the sleeve notes of the album, as well as thanking his childhood sweetheart Kara ('the cabbage patch kid') and Michael Jackson himself, James had a message for someone particularly important to the success of this record.

'Tom Fletcher,' he wrote, 'sometimes I wonder how many fish there really are swimming around in that pond we both know about. All I can say is that if we keep on fishing there together, we're gonna catch 'em all! You are a great fisherman and I can't wait for the world to hear the McFly album.'

The world couldn't wait either. But it had a good few months yet before the album would be available to buy. In the meantime, the McFly boys were teasing their public with some tantalising performances – including their first, in December 2003, on *CD:UK*, the popular Saturday-morning music show that regularly attracted more than 2 million viewers. Two million viewers? It was quite a big deal for the boys' first ever TV appearance.

At least they had some friends on hand to help them through it. James, Matt and Charlie appeared on the show on the same day, and they went first, performing 'Who's David?', which was due to be released in February 2004 as the second single from *A Present for Everyone*. It was another Bourne–Fletcher collaboration and was a ballad with balls, as was always Busted's way.

As James started singing, the fans around him cheered deliriously, and he somewhat self-consciously acknowledged them. It still didn't feel real to him that this was his life: performing to adoring fans, being loved in return. Matt, meanwhile – for once with rather plain dark hair – gave a typically spirited performance. His voice, which had just got better and better, beat the hell out of the middle-eight section. It had a gorgeous rasp to it, and the more heartfelt lyric of this song, with its pleading narrative to an unfaithful girlfriend, suited his tone perfectly.

At the end of their performance, James took the mic. He waited for the screaming to die down and then said, 'OK, I'm extremely excited right now, 'cause right now it's time to introduce a few buddies of mine.' The girls, already wound up by Busted's performance, just screamed harder. Matt came up behind James, having crossed from the other side of the stage, to be present at this momentous occasion. He patted James on the back a couple of times and delivered a classic gurn to the camera. James leaned into the lens, too.

'In the words of Marty McFly: you guys might not be ready for this yet, but your kids are going to love it.'

He looked excited just to be saying those words. As Harry's drumsticks started pounding the skins, James yelled, 'Put your hands together for McFly!' And the soon-to-be iconic bass line rang out around the studio, as '5 Colours in Her Hair' made its debut to the nation.

The boys must have been nervous, but they didn't look it. Not one bit. Danny had the tough job of taking the first line, yet he delivered it with all the swagger of a Gallagher brother, his arm held confidently high when he wasn't playing his guitar. All of them were dressed in vibrant colours – Tom in acid yellow and Dougie in neon orange – and it looked like a bright new dawn of pop music.

They were an instant hit. They were so confident – having spent months rehearsing together, as tight-knit onstage as they were chilling in their shared house – that that first performance had all the hallmarks of what would become classic McFly, Danny and Dougie sharing a mic as they crooned the catchy song together; Danny leaping up to play in front of Harry's drum kit as Tom took over lead vocals. This was so clearly not a manufactured band: these were four true friends, having the time of their lives.

And they had two other friends who wanted to congratulate them too. James and Matt, along with Charlie, stormed the stage at the close of the performance. James and Tom high-fived each other instantly, their delight writ clear across their faces, before Charlie – Tom's collaborator on 'That Thing You Do', the song that had started this whole sound – pulled him into a bear hug. Matt punched the air with sheer joy. And James just managed to high-five

These were four true friends, having the time of their lives

Danny before the Northern lad spotted pretty presenter Cat Deeley, and swooped in, in a very Danny way, to steal a kiss from her. 'Thank you,' he said. 'Absolute quality!'

He was talking about the performance, and James had a few words to say, too. When Cat asked him how proud he was of his friends right now, on a scale of one to ten, his answer was swift and sure. 'Oh, ten. Ten out of ten.'

Yet it was two out of three who appeared on Frank Skinner's ITV show later that month when Busted, who were now at the fame and popularity level of top chat-show guests, were invited on just before Christmas. Charlie was unwell, so only James and Matt sat on the sofa. It looked odd, the duo together. There was something about the triumvirate that worked, and they looked somehow lopsided without their taller bandmate. Imbalanced.

Matt was certainly knocked sideways when Skinner introduced his former teacher Ms Blair – the inspiration for Miss Mackenzie in 'What I Go to School For' – who was in the audience. He blushed as red as Skinner's sofas, though Frank perhaps summed up best what everyone was thinking when he said of the attractive teacher, 'I see what you mean, though.'

Skinner held up the band's CD onscreen, hoping to sell a few more albums for the lads as festive gifts before the year was out. Busted were almost the bestselling British group of 2003, second only to Coldplay; a couple more sales would boost them even higher.

If Frank had opened the plastic case, he would have seen a very exciting announcement. In spring 2004, from 26 February, Busted were headlining their first ever arena tour. There was a leaflet inside the CD promoting the tour – and the support act.

McFly and Busted were hitting the road together for the very first time.

And it wouldn't be the last.

SIX

Up All Night

It was 14 February 2004 – twelve days before the massive arena tour kicked off. Twenty-four mammoth gigs nationwide awaited the seven hungry-for-it lads. One whole month of performing, touring, and of course, partying.

But before all that there was the little matter of Valentine's Day. For Tom, recently reunited with Giovanna, what better gift for the maker of a number-one hit to give his girlfriend than a song written all about her?

'All About You' was written by Tom in about five minutes flat, recorded as a favour by Danny in his home recording studio and then delivered, by hand, by Tom himself later that same night. It was the first time, other than his early attempts when he was learning how to structure songs, that Tom had written a song without James, Dougie or Danny. This one was just for Gi.

Before the tour kicked off, Fletch had a serious chat with his new young stars. Well, by 'serious chat' read 'complete and utter bollocking to end all bollockings'. He'd found out about the dope smoking, and he wasn't impressed. The guys were read the riot act – Tom never touched drugs again – and it wasn't something Harry was going to forget in a hurry. He said in *Unsaid Things,*

Tom never touched drugs again

> From day one our managers were a hell of a sight tougher with McFly than they ever were with Busted ... For Fletch and Richard, Busted were a bit like guinea pigs for how they would manage McFly. Busted had their problems. They didn't always see eye to eye ... Whether or not Fletch and Richard thought this was anything to do with their rock 'n' roll lifestyle, I don't know. But once Matt and Charlie started going down that road, it was already out of their management's control.

And, for the arena tour, Matt Willis in particular planned to party as uncontrollably as possible. His affinity with alcohol hadn't gone unnoticed by the fans. Themed gifts would arrive for him, such as key rings with the slogan 'Pissed and Happy' and badges with the monikers 'Beer Monster' and 'Mine's a Pint'. One fan created a home-made 'Busted Fan Annual 2003–2004', which included pictures of the band at their BRIT Awards triumph on 17 February. The two images were captioned, respectively: '1 p.m. – Sober' and '1 a.m. – Drunk'.

In the boys' defence, the BRITs marked a pretty momentous

day. They'd been nominated for three awards; they won two. Busted were officially the Best British Breakthrough and the Best Pop act in the country, and they only narrowly missed out on Best British Group when the Darkness pipped them to the post. The prestigious awards demonstrated genuine respect and recognition for their talents, and they meant a lot to the band. For, despite the fact that they'd desecrated the former model of pop, which had featured squeaky-clean boy bands such as Westlife and a rabid invasion of reality-TV stars, there were some who tried to dismiss Busted as gimmicky pop – even labelling them as 'just another boy band'.

James was quick to challenge such claims in no uncertain terms. 'We write the songs, we sing the songs, we play the instruments, and, if that's not credible enough, then f**k off!' And Matt would say jokingly on their documentary series *America or Busted*, 'Do I dance? Do I wear sequins? No.'

Charlie, however, found it harder to get over the unfair labelling, saying frankly on *America or Busted*, 'The whole boy-band thing, it really f**ked me off.' Asked by journalist Peter Robinson about Busted breaking America – they would have a TV crew following them later in the year, making the fly-on-the-wall programme *America or Busted*, as they took their songs Stateside – Charlie responded passionately. 'For me,' he said, 'I don't want to have to fight the same old battles that we fought in the UK. I don't want the same old bullshit trying to convince people that we're not idiots.'

Idiots or not, hundreds of thousands of people wanted to see them play live. Demand was such that a second tour was already set up for the autumn. Busted would eventually sell out an unprecedented eleven Wembley dates in 2004, and gain a new record as the band to play the most consecutive dates at the iconic venue, which held 12,500 screaming fans. At Wembley alone, they'd be playing to almost 140,000 people.

But before Wembley came Dublin, and the first night of the joint Busted–McFly tour, on Thursday, 26 February. The venue was the Point, Ireland's premier arena. McFly's debut gig was going to be in front of thousands of people – yet that wasn't what Tom was really stoked about. As he recalled in *Unsaid Things*, 'Matt Willis's seal of approval on our McFly material meant everything to me. A complimentary word from him meant more to me than from anyone else.' And, with Matt backing McFly as his support act, it was about the biggest vote of confidence he could give.

As for Matt himself, he couldn't wait to get started. He told Peter Robinson, 'This is what it's all been about. This is what being in Busted is *all* about. Playing live is everything.'

As the lights dipped, at 7.30 p.m. on the dot, screams erupted in the arena. Onstage, Danny psyched himself up. Dougie pulled on his bass-guitar strap. Tom swallowed hard. And Harry tried to get over his disappointment that the screams weren't *quite* as ear-blasting as he'd been anticipating. He lifted his drumsticks to count in the band. A-one, two, a-one-two . . .

And McFly launched into their opening number, 'Saturday Night', with its explosive guitar intro to rival Marty McFly ripping off Chuck Berry. It was the kind of moment Danny Jones had been dreaming of in Bolton ever since he'd first picked up an instrument aged six. The Busted fans went wild.

Backstage, Matt pricked up his ears. 'Listen to that,' he

commented to James. 'They're going to be screaming for us later.'

McFly's set was only five songs long. 'Down by the Lake' followed 'Saturday Night', and then they launched into 'Obviously', written by James, Danny and Tom only eight months before. They paid homage to the Beatles with

Listen to that: they're going to be screaming for us later

a cover of 'She Loves You', and then finished with what was fast becoming their signature tune, '5 Colours in Her Hair'. A local reporter from the BBC commented, 'I've never seen a crowd get into support acts so much – they loved them. Everyone was on their feet singing away to the infectious "5 Colours in Her Hair".'

Even Matt Willis couldn't help but notice the incredible reaction. Speaking in a McFly VT years later, he said, 'McFly had something immediately. As soon as you saw them play live, they had something that [even] Busted didn't have, actually, which was genuine, between all four of them: they were just like brothers. They had this bond.' And the close friendships between Tom, Danny, Dougie and Harry were only cemented further as they shared the surreal experience of that debut show. Dripping with sweat, the McFly boys came excitedly off the stage, grins pasted widely on each of their happy faces, just as Busted were warming up for the main event.

If possible, the screams got even louder when the lights dipped for the third time that night (Prestige had also booked V, the band Danny didn't join, as a support act for the tour). And the lights stayed off. The Busted boys got into place in the darkness. And then, through the massive speakers, throughout the pitch-black hall, the unmistakeable bass of 'Air Hostess' began. *Do do do do do do do do . . .* In a sudden blaze of light, the band appeared mysteriously from below the stage straight onto it – and then they were off. Matt said in *Busted on Tour*, 'We totally knew from the word go that "Air Hostess" had to be the opening track, if only for the amazing intro.'

It was an amazing introduction to the whole show, let alone the song. The Busted boys were at their best throughout, dashing off guitar riffs and spunky banter as though they were born to do it. They threw themselves about with an incredible energy that unwittingly revealed the enormous amounts of Haribo sweets they'd consumed before the gig. The signature Busted move – knee-high jumps *avec* guitars – was rocked again and again, as the boys bounced about the stage like space hoppers.

After the show, the whole tour crew headed to Lillie's Bordello, Dublin's leading nightclub, situated at the bottom of Grafton Street. Amid scenes of much celebration, a toast was raised to the first night of a very, very special tour. To V. To McFly. To Busted. To the band. As the seven friends buzzed on the adrenaline of the arena show and the best booze Lillie's Bordello could offer, they excitedly shared memories of their time onstage and began a bond that would last much, much longer than that first round of drinks.

From then on, the booze – and the friendship – didn't stop flowing. The Belfast gigs saw all three bands sitting in a huge circle necking drinks until 3 a.m. Matt would later say to Fearne Cotton on *Fearne and McBusted*, 'The second Busted tour? I can't even really remember being on it.'

Luckily for him, Busted had a book deal, and journalist Peter

Robinson had the enviable job of following the boys around on each and every gig – an 'access all areas' pass that produced the book *Busted on Tour*. Night after night, Matt's drunken exploits are recorded: mixing his usual 'cocktail' of every drink under the sun at Tiger Tiger in Manchester; having more wild nights out with Lee Ryan; filling hotel corridors with smoke as he and his musician mates stayed up jamming till 4 a.m., the vapours seeping out from under his room door until the whole passageway was fully fumigated.

I threw a television out a window

But, even by Matt's impressive standards, on Monday, 7 March, he really outdid himself. Matt later told the story to Fearne Cotton in her TV documentary, surrounded by sniggering Tom, Dougie, Harry and Danny:

I threw a television out a window. I was kind of provoked though. I was in a hotel room with an *NME* journalist. They were like, 'This is pretty lame,' and I was like, 'Well, I'll throw a telly out the window then' . . . and I did. I threw it out the window, and outside the window was our tour bus. It went just the other side of the tour bus . . . and exploded on the street. It made such a big noise. It sounded like a bomb had gone off. Me and the journalist ran away.

When we went back in, the police were there. They were going to take me to the police station, but then our tour manager sweet-talked the policewoman with some tickets and a meet-and-greet for the next night.

So the next day suddenly I was standing there and there was the policewoman with her kids: 'Hi, Matt! Can we have a picture?'

And I was like, 'Yep!'

The *Sun* reported that, he followed up the telly with a toaster, something they were very disparaging about – apparently, domestic appliances are not rock 'n' roll. According to the *Sun*, they're 'well, domestic'.

As usual, Tom and James were marking the tour in a very different way. Their late-night writing sessions were just as regular as they had been the year before on Busted's theatre tour, and just as much fun for the two mates – though the hits may have been fewer, with one creation called 'The Girl from the Fit Girls' Table'. It wasn't quite as catchy as 'Crashed the Wedding'.

James revealed some of their songwriting secrets to Peter Robinson. It turned out that Matt and Danny weren't the only Oasis fans on the tour. While they may have launched their respective careers with their performances of 'Don't Look Back in Anger' in their local pubs, for James it was all about 'Wonderwall'. He said, 'One of the first songs I learned was "Wonderwall" by Oasis. And, if you listen to them, you'll notice that a lot of our songs use the same technique as "Wonderwall". Noel Gallagher will probably hate that – but it's his music that inspired us.'

Just being on tour was pretty inspirational too. Harry, Dougie, Danny, Tom, Matt and James were having the time of their lives. Every night, they would eat together in catering, put on the show of their lives and then party till the small hours – whenever McFly were allowed to stay up late (Fletch was still keeping them on a super-short leash). Harry would later say to *Attitude* magazine, 'We weren't even allowed to hang out with Matt; he was such a live wire.'

They were also recording together. McFly's debut single was due for release just after the tour finished, on 29 March, and Busted and McFly planned another B-side to die for – this time a cover of the Kinks' 'Lola', first released in 1970.

As you might expect for a cover on a McFly rather than a Busted single, the track begins in a slightly less punk and more gentle way than their previous collaboration on 'Build Me Up Buttercup': just an acoustic guitar and Tom's pleasant vocals. But then that infectious bass line and Harry's drums kick in, along with the other boys' drawling, more rocky voices and those all-important guitars, and the pace picks up. It's a track that builds and builds. By the time the bridge is reached around two minutes in, it's a veritable singalong of a song. You can almost imagine the campfire the band might be gathered around, with Danny, Tom and James strumming their guitars casually by the light of the dying embers; Matt and Dougie smouldering in the background as they pick out the notes on the bass. It was a more laid-back track overall – more a recording of a jamming session than a stand-out single – yet it still had that unique energy that irrepressibly came through whenever the two bands joined forces.

The B-side had an unexpected downside, however. Already closely linked with Busted, due to their shared management and their obvious friendship, McFly found themselves lumbered with the label 'Busted Juniors'. For the four boys, especially Tom and Danny who had pioneered the McFly sound – albeit with James – it was a tough tag. They were their own band. Even some of

Harry's old Uppingham school friends jumped on the band-wagon, ribbing him that McFly were just the same as Busted. They came up with what they thought of as a hilarious nickname for his new band, with which they used to take the mick out of him mercilessly. The name? McBusted.

James was quick to defend McFly, and the new friends he'd made in every member of the band, in *Busted on Tour*:

> **They came up with what they thought of as a hilarious nickname for his new band: McBusted**

As similar as some people might think the two bands are, we're not that similar at all. McFly is completely inspired by sixties and sometimes fifties music. There are chords you'd use in a McFly song, which you'd never use in a Busted song. It's only because we introduced McFly that people think we're similar . . . I think McFly is a good thing for Busted. Forget my involvement with their songs – McFly are simply very good.

And the public were with him all the way. '5 Colours in Her Hair' went straight to number one. Busted may have made *Guinness World Records* with their slow but steady delivery of 3-2-1 hits, but McFly were showing them how it was really done by heading to the top of the charts on their very first try.

And they were even gaining critical acclaim too. The *Observer* described the song as 'undeniably infectious' while the BBC called it a 'striking chart-topper'. And it was a toe-tapping gift of a tune.

Inspired by the Beach Boys' surf vibe, it had a cool, refreshing sound in an era when Victoria Beckham was making the charts as a solo artist and Michelle McManus and 'Sam and Mark' from *Pop Idol* were hitting the top ten. And when the boys had recorded the single, they'd left the tape running at the end of the take. The authenticity of Danny's post-song exclamation, his Bolton accent coming out thickly as he said, 'Did you hear my voice?' about the high notes, just made them sound even more credible. It felt as if he were just jamming with his mates, with Tom and Harry and Dougie in the studio; listeners could actually hear the laughter of the four friends, who were quite simply having fun while making music.

And while those four friends may not have loved their first video – which saw them playing a gig on a *Top of the Pops*-style set circa 1964, messing about with surfboards, walking along the Abbey Road crossing *à la* the Beatles, and encouraging a girl in a black-and-white world to join their über-colourful TV set – it actually encapsulated their sixties-inspired song pretty well. They could at least count themselves lucky in one regard. The video introduced them to the world with their names onscreen next to their faces. When Universal had done something similar with Busted on the 'You Said No' video, James Bourne had been transformed into 'James Harris' and the video shown on TV before anyone noticed the clanger. This time, all the names were present and correct; in fact, the director made a joke of it by making Dougie and Danny ensure their names were in the right place.

For McFly, topping the charts was a strange anticlimax. Though Fletch turned up with a video camera to film the momentous occasion when they heard the news, and the boys obligingly cheered enthusiastically, Tom recalled in *Unsaid Things*, 'We were a bit oblivious to it all. Nobody else around us made much of a fuss about being number one. Busted had already been there and done that, remember. I guess it wasn't so exciting to have us coming along and doing it second.'

Of course, this being the McFly and Busted boys, they still celebrated. James and some other mates came round to the Finchley pad for a good old knees-up. Congratulations banners were pinned to the walls, where they cohabited with the strings of fairy lights. There was booze. Tom and James each grabbed a champagne bottle and tried to release the corks simultaneously. A snapshot in McFly's autobiography shows them, mouths wide open and bottles pointed like pistols, about to

> **Tom and James each grabbed a champagne bottle**

set them off. It was a moment to remember. And for James it was a fitting climax to the end of the shared tour. He said in *Busted on Tour*, 'I'm not really an "emotional last night" type of person, but I enjoyed soaking up that feeling for one last time. As soon as I get out of bed tomorrow there will still be a million other things going on, and there'll be a million other things the day after that. But I'm never going to forget this tour.'

Busy toasting McFly's number one, the boys didn't get much sleep that night.

And Charlie wasn't getting much sleep, either. He told Peter Robinson that he'd been plagued by dreams throughout the tour. Of getting shot. Of being electrocuted. 'The blood,' he confessed, 'always feels really warm.'

Charlie probably didn't set much store by dream dictionaries. He probably never looked up what his dreams might mean. Had he done so, he might have seen this definition on DreamMoods.com:

To dream that you are shot or being shot at represents a form of self-punishment that you may be subconsciously imposing on yourself. You may have done something that you are ashamed of or are not proud of. If you are shot and come back as a different person, then it indicates that you need to start fresh. You want to wipe the past away and literally become a new person.

As for being electrocuted?

'To dream of an electrocution indicates that the current course of your actions . . . will lead to disaster.'

SEVEN

Party's Over

On a corner of Chalk Farm Road, in London's grungy Camden district, sits the Barfly pub, home to alternative rock gigs, indie music and occasional pop. It was used to playing host to bands such as the Killers, who'd released their debut album *Hot Fuss* in the June of 2004, and the Strokes. On the evening of Wednesday, 14 July 2004, McFly were on the bill. And the 200 fans who'd got golden tickets to the intimate gig were about to witness a moment in music history.

McFly's debut album, *Room on the 3rd Floor*, had been released a week earlier. Onstage that night at the Barfly, Danny, Tom, Dougie and Harry were presented with an award from *Guinness World Records*. They had overtaken the Beatles to become the youngest band ever to have an album debut at number one. Tom was about to turn nineteen – his birthday was that coming

Saturday – Danny and Harry were eighteen, and Dougie was just sixteen.

They'd shifted more than 60,000 copies of their debut in a single week, and garnered the kind of critical acclaim that they'd dreamed of, back when they were writing songs in James's flat and in that now-famous room on the third floor at the InterContinental. The *Observer* wrote, 'These are immaculately constructed pop songs articulating genuine teenage emotions . . . *Room on the 3rd Floor* is a delicious blend of fantasy and reality: classic pop storytelling, with some brilliant handclaps.' And if the critics did insist on referencing Busted in their reviews ('Their mentors, Busted, have remoulded the fresh putty of American pop-punk into something that still sounds new. McFly's influences are ancient in comparison, making the end product sound rather retrospective. But that's not to say it's a bad record,' wrote the BBC, rather half-heartedly), well, McFly weren't above referencing them, either.

They knew exactly who they wanted to thank for their success. Writing in the sleeve notes of the album, every single member of the band, in his individual acknowledgements, name-checked James and Matt, and the whole band wrote, 'Special thanks to our writing mate James Bourne, along with Charley [sic] and Matt of Busted, who not only helped launch our career but have been our friends and advisers.' And James in particular was singled out. 'James, you psychedelic love child, thanks so much for everything. Man, it's been fun so far, huh?' wrote Harry; 'James – without you we wouldn't have so many

James, you psychedelic love child

killer chunes!' from Dougie; while Danny simply wrote, 'James Bourne "ya nimpty" you simply are a legend at songwriting. You're a top mate.' The unique friendships between the two bands, forged in the fire of that spring arena tour and in song-writing sessions from the previous summer, had blossomed into proper bromance territory.

For Tom, whose partnership with James had started the whole enterprise, it was an opportunity to celebrate him in print. 'James Bourne, you dude!' he began. 'Thank you so much! You taught me everything I know about fishing, dude, and we caught some big ones last year. It's a big ocean out there ...'

A big ocean – but a small world. The Barfly was also the venue for the first gigs of Charlie Simpson's new band, Fightstar, who were cranking up their activity, writing songs and playing gigs, as 2004 whizzed by.

It was incredible that Charlie found the time to do both. Both Busted and McFly were dominating the charts across the world; and Tom and James's songs were also finding a life outside the two bands. In May, the Prestige-managed boy band V had launched their debut single with a B-side of none other than 'Chills in the Evening', the very first song Tom and James had written together. The single got to number six, and it was billed as a 'V featuring McFly' B-side. Danny did get to perform with V after all, on *CD:UK*, delivering a stunning guitar solo while the boy-band members crooned somewhat awkwardly around him. McFly were set on raised stages behind the five-piece – and they really were on another level.

Throughout that year, McFly totted up top hits at a rate of knots: 'Obviously' in June; 'That Girl' in September; 'Room on the 3rd Floor' in November. And Busted were doing the same: 'Who's David?' went to number one in February; 'Air Hostess' to number two in April; and the double A-side of 'Thunderbirds Are Go'/'3am' to number one in July, just a couple of weeks after McFly's Barfly gig.

And new songs needed new videos. Matt wasn't always impressed with the treatments, though, as he told Peter Robinson, after he had to film scenes for 'Who's David?' in the same phone box as he'd used for the 'Sleeping with the Light On' video. He said, 'It did rather seem as if someone had decided that, whenever Busted do a song which isn't about air hostesses getting off with teachers at a wedding in the year 3000, I have to stand looking pensive in a phone box. Not just [any] phone box. The phone box. The Matt from Busted Phone Box of Moodiness.'

Still, he had his own way of coping. As he later told Fearne Cotton, 'If I wanted to drink at 10 o'clock at a shoot, I bloody would.' And he did. It didn't seem to occur to him to stop, or that it was an extraordinary thing to be boozing before noon. For Matt, it was a way of life. He would drink as soon as he woke up. He would drink a 'liquid lunch'. He would drink before gigs in the evenings, to take the edge off his nerves. He drank to socialise, to function and to survive. And all that alcohol was garnished by the grass of his daily spliffs. No one said no. No one said stop. And Matt had never been one to live life with any kind of caution anyway: he was an all-or-nothing guy. Busted's success had given him money to burn – and, in a sense, he did that every time he touched his lighter to his roll-up, or chain-smoked another ciggie in a bar, nursing just one more drink between his nicotine-flavoured fingers, as he sipped greedily and with untethered joy at the glass. He was a happy drunk, and nothing made him happier than swinging into a brand-new bar and ordering yet another drink.

And there were more excuses to raise a glass come the summer. In August, following a final UK gig in Swansea, Busted headed off to try to break America. Matt had just turned twenty-one – the legal age for consuming alcohol in the States – so for him it was perfect timing. And for James, too, it was a good time to get away, as he and Kara had called time on their relationship after almost seven years together. The break-up was amicable enough, but it was still hard to adjust to life without her – particularly because Matt was beginning to share some of his nights out with a girl who was turning out to be pretty special, though it would be a while before they officially got together.

Life in Busted, and now in McFly, too, involved a chaotic round of interviews. Radio 1, *Smash Hits*, MTV ... And it was at MTV that Matt Willis first met a young presenter called Emma Griffiths. She was a twenty-eight-year-old former model from Sutton Coldfield, who had recently moved into TV presenting. Very pretty, with a relaxed vibe in front of the camera and a lovely jokey manner, she and Matt were kindred spirits, bantering back and forth both on- and offscreen.

For McFly, though they knew the round of interviews was necessary, like Busted before them they found the boy-band tag that accompanied the teen magazines irritating. Alexis Petridis, a *Guardian* journalist who spent time with them that summer, observed of them at a *Smash Hits* shoot, 'On command, they adopt their trademark facial expression: a sort of perplexed, bug-eyed sneer that implies they have merely popped out for a pint of milk, become involved in an inexplicable chain of misunder-standings and now find themselves being photographed for the cover of a teen magazine with an enormous glittery heart by mistake.'

Yet the serious music press – who had responded rather well to Busted when they first burst onto the music scene, albeit with a few 'boy band' digs – were more resistant to the 'Busted Juniors', as they perceived them. The NME, in particular, launched a vicious attack on the teenagers, captioning one picture of the foursome, 'From left to right: C**t, Wanker, Dickhead and Twat.' Their fans might adore them (a selection of banners recalled by Harry included HARRY, BANG ME LIKE YOU BANG YOUR DRUMS, DO ME DOUGIE-STYLE and DANNY, LET ME UNZIP YOUR McFLY) but the world at large still had reservations.

I hate feeling like we're being pushed into doing something that we don't want to do

Busted were hoping the American trip would give them a chance to start from scratch. Yet when they heard their US label's plans for them, which included the usual teen press rather than the music media, their hearts sank. Charlie sounded a word of warning on America or Busted: 'I hate feeling like we're being pushed into doing something that we don't want to do. I'll end up thinking, I don't want to f**king be here . . .'

As the year drew to a close, both bands were touring: Busted with another arena tour, and that incredible number of sold-out Wembley gigs; McFly on their first headlining theatre tour. Busted found time to record the Band Aid 20 single in November, appearing alongside Bono, Chris Martin and Paul McCartney on the classic 'Do They Know It's Christmas?' It would become the biggest-selling record of 2004 and the Christmas number one. And it also led to an opportunity for McFly: 'All About You' was selected as the Comic Relief single for the coming spring. No wonder Dougie was celebrating. As he turned seventeen on 30 November, he started enjoying a nice glass or two of red wine.

For Matt, there was a lot to look forward to. He said in *Busted*, 'I've got a lot of things to do in life . . . I want to be able to look back in ten years, having released eight albums, and go, "Look at that. Look what I've done."' Their backers certainly thought they had it in them. Mishal Varma, vice-president of network programming at MTV Asia, told Peter Robinson: 'We're expecting them to be a really big act over here for the next few years.'

Surveying the thousands upon thousands of fans at Wembley Arena on Saturday, 18 December, on the final night of the 2004 Busted tour, it seemed certain that the band were here to stay. James, Matt and Charlie broke into 'Year 3000' at the very end of the encore and it seemed possible that they would still be singing their hearts out in that infamous year itself. James, hearing his own lyrics about his favourite film sung back to him by the fans, was genuinely moved. Performing live was what he lived for. He told Peter Robinson, 'The funny thing, and the thing that some people don't realise, is that when we're onstage we have as good a time, if not a better time, than the fans do. That's just the way it is. If they want us here, we'll be here. We're not ready for a farewell tour.

'We haven't even really begun yet.'

As the final thrum of the guitars on 'Year 3000' faded into the frantic screaming of the fans, James laid down his guitar and headed offstage.

The tour might be over, but he knew he had plenty more to give.

Six days later, it was Christmas Eve. And Charlie Simpson had a very important meeting with his management. He had only one thing to say.

He was leaving Busted.

James was snowboarding with his family. He didn't know a thing. Later, on *The Jonathan Ross Show*, he said, 'People didn't tell me because I would have been the most sad.' He recalled on *Fearne and McBusted*, 'At one point my dad pulled me aside and he just said . . . "The whole thing's over." I think everyone knew except for me. I was shocked.'

'Shocked' doesn't really cover it. This was a bombshell. Matt Willis had had an inkling something was up, later telling The Vault, 'I saw it coming if I'm honest. I thought it was going to happen before it did.' He said to FleckingRecords.co.uk, 'To be honest, Charlie made the last year of Busted pretty miserable for me.' He later went even further, in a drunken interview with VJ Scorpio TV.

The whole thing's over

Clutching a bottle of beer, he revealed, 'Charlie was into [Fightstar] . . . He didn't give a f**k . . . James hated him for being in Fightstar. And Charlie hated him for hating him for being in Fightstar. But it was never said. So therefore I was the bitch in the middle . . . In the end I just got pissed.' More and more often, that was becoming Matt's answer to everything.

James elaborated on the tension between him and Charlie on *Fearne and McBusted*: 'I never went to his Fightstar shows because I never really felt welcome . . . He never invited me personally to a gig.' And Matt added to Fearne, 'Charlie wanted to lead the direction of the band, but James was the backbone of the direction of the band. That's probably where things went a bit wrong. I think Charlie started to hate Busted, and what Busted stood for. He didn't have much control on where the band was going and I think in the end that ate him up. He was just not into it.'

James continued, 'I definitely understood his desire to make music that he believed in and wanted to do – because that's what I want to do.'

But he wasn't going to be able to do it any more. On Thursday, 13 January, the band called a crisis meeting. James and Matt were still shell-shocked by Charlie's decision. They had always, always said that if one of them left the others wouldn't continue as a duo. Busted was over.

Friday, 14 January 2005. It wasn't a particularly chilly day – it was a mild 8 degrees Celsius on the bustling London streets outside – but the atmosphere inside the stunned press-conference room at the Soho Hotel was as cold as ice. Amid a cacophony of calls from the waiting journalists and a blizzard of camera flashes, the three men slowly made their way into the room, about to deliver the worst news of two of their young lives. Charlie sat in the middle, with James to his right and Matt to his left. James wore a black baseball cap that shadowed his eyes, but his open mouth showcased just how jaw-dropping the news had been to him. He looked as if he was still in shock.

Charlie, whose decision had prompted the conference, spoke first. 'As a lot of you know, there's been a lot of speculation in the past month about the future of this band. We want to set the record straight now. So, with that in mind, I am here to tell you that I've quit Busted.' His voice, that plummy yet gravelly drawl that fans the world over adored, sounded taut with tension. 'I've been slightly concerned that I've been reading things in the press. It's been saying that the band hasn't got on and that I've been embarrassed to be in Busted. I want to completely quash those rumours because I've had the most amazing three years. These two' – and he gestured at Matt and James sitting either side of him – 'have been absolutely amazing. Two of my best friends and amazing bandmates. And I wish them all the best in the future.'

James, who looked as if he was struggling to keep the tears inside, spoke next. 'We want Busted to be remembered as the three of us. And, that way [not continuing], it will always be the three of us. No one's going to try and carry anything on.' His last word was for all those who had embraced his songs, his lyrics – his world. 'I want to thank the fans. They're awesome.'

And then there was only Matt left to speak: 'James has been my best friend for [four] years ... this is a really hard time for us.' Magnanimously, he wished Charlie well with the new band.

And then the three former Busted boys rose from their chairs, and left the press conference room behind them.

James and Matt wouldn't speak to Charlie again for seven years.

Almost four years to the day since Matt had first knocked on James's door in Southend-on-Sea, it was just the two of them again. From those humble beginnings, they had conquered the world. But now it was all just ashes. And there was no time-travelling car coming to save them. No 'To be continued . . .'

Only: The End.

In a studio across town, the McFly boys heard the news as they filmed the video to 'All About You'. Now, it really was. Busted were out of the game – and McFly were on their own.

Tom recalled in *Unsaid Things*, 'Seeing [Busted] split was a reminder of how lucky we were that the four of us were so close. I wish that had stuck with me over the months that were to come.'

That was because, as Tom's star was in the ascendant as part of McFly, his spirits were plummeting to rock bottom. He was moody, depressed, low. The world

Busted were out of the game – and McFly were on their own

seemed bleak. He and Giovanna had a rocky time around then, but they got through it. He should have been on top of the world. Instead, inside, in his very core, everything was black and cold.

To the outside world, McFly were bigger than ever. In February 2005 they completed the baton handover initiated by the Busted split by taking home the BRIT Award for Best Pop act – the award Busted had so excitedly claimed just a year before. They announced that they would be in a Hollywood movie with Lindsay Lohan, to be filmed that same year. They even starred in British favourite *Casualty*. And they jetted to New Orleans to work on songs for the film.

It was while they were in New Orleans, just before the BRITs, that Danny got a call from his sister Vicky. She told him their dad was having an affair. Danny flew home to support his mum and try to reason with his dad. But his parents' relationship was over. He later said to the *Daily Mail*, 'I hate thinking about it. My dad went off with another woman. It was a weak mid-life-crisis thing – he just left us. I think he's a prat and I'd never do what he did. In the end I had to pay him off. I don't want to see him again.'

With Danny reeling from his dad's betrayal – a reaction with which Dougie could wholly sympathise, after his father's actions just eighteen months before – and Tom feeling low, the band's second album was going to be much, much darker than their debut. How could it not be? Songwriters feed off the world around them. And, while Danny may have hated thinking about his dad, he was able to channel the experience into music. 'The Ballad of Paul K' was written by the band about his and Dougie's dads leaving, and 'Don't Know Why', which Danny wrote with his sister Vicky, explored the dark theme of their father's treachery. Later, when he'd perform 'Don't Know Why' onstage, his face supersized on the big screens, he'd have a faraway look in his eyes. Maybe remembering.

The Bourne–Fletcher duo had a track on the album, the yearning 'Memory Lane'. The record also featured an entirely orchestral track, an incredible achievement for a so-called 'boy band', which formed part one of 'She Falls Asleep', a song about teenage suicide. It was a bleak album for what had seemed pop's brightest shining lights.

And for Matt Willis, too, times were very, very dark. In Busted, he drank to celebrate. Now, he drank to forget that his dreams lay shattered; to forget that the band was over. According to a 'close pal' of his who was quoted in the *Mirror*, 'Matt probably took the break-up of the band the hardest. He was left with too much time on his hands and lots of mates who wanted to drag him to the nearest bar.' Matt himself said to EDP24.com, the web presence of the *Eastern Daily Press*, 'I was pretty upset about it all. I was down about it and it drove me crazy. I'm not very good left to my own devices. I get into trouble.'

Trouble before the band had split had meant too many wild nights out and raucous carryings-on. Now, the daily drinking that had previously buoyed him up through the non-stop schedule of being in a band, powering him through the photoshoots and live performances, became a life raft in his darkest hour. Too late, he realised that the life raft was pulling him under. He had a problem. He knew he did. He later said to the *Mirror*, 'It was awful. I was very unhappy and probably in the lowest point of my life. I hit self-destruct mode. When you're told to f**king look at the rest of your life at twenty-one, it's a bit worrying when you don't see anything.'

Emma Griffiths, who was now his girlfriend, dropped him off at the Priory rehab clinic just months after Busted split, so he could seek help for his alcohol addiction. She was reportedly

I hit self-destruct mode

the only person allowed to stay in contact with him during his time there. The 'close pal' in the *Mirror* continued, 'Matt's phone is turned off and no one can get hold of him. Obviously, James is really worried about him, but Matt's therapists think isolation is for the best. The only person he has allowed to visit him is Emma.'

It was an experience that brought the young couple closer together. As Matt later revealed in an interview with Sing365.com, 'In rehab you've got nothing except coffee ... Everyone wants a luxury, and mine was the thought of my girl-friend driving me home.' Yet she came to pick him up a bit earlier than expected.

Matt, having sorted out his head, quit the rehab course after just two weeks of a month-long treatment programme. He was fine, he thought. It had all been a bit of an overreaction. To Sing365.com, he said, 'In rehab, they talk about you hitting rock bottom, but I saw it more as prevention against becoming a total arsehole. I did the whole going-to-meetings thing, I stopped drinking for a while ... but I listened to everyone talk about how dark it was and I was like, "Wait a second, I had a wicked time!"'

And someone who was happy to join him for a drink was Dougie Poynter, who'd now upgraded from the red wine and was enjoying the cool charms of Russian vodka.

James, who'd never made a habit of drowning his sorrows in the first place, had to find another outlet for his pain at Busted's break-up.

He knew only one thing that would make him feel better.

He was going to start another band.

EIGHT

Walk in the Sun

'So ... who's most looking forward to meeting Lindsay Lohan?' Cat Deeley asked McFly one Saturday morning on the set of *CD:UK*.

In a heartbeat, Harry Judd's arm shot straight into the air, a good two seconds before his bandmates reacted. When Cat asked if any of the McFly boys fancied Lindsay, Harry replied with typical cockiness, 'No, apparently she fancies us, though.'

His jokey reply wasn't far from his mind as Hollywood actress Lindsay Lohan opened the door to her hotel room late one night during the filming of *Just My Luck* – and invited him inside. Never, in a million years, did he ever think he'd be making out with a movie star – even if she would later deny that anything had taken place.

Speaking to the *Mirror*, he revealed the vital statistics of their night of passion together by saying, 'At the time I thought, "This is awesome," but I was really nervous. Lindsay invited me back to her hotel ... I didn't shag her, but we spent the night and had a fumble ... We did things teenagers do. We went far enough but not the full home run.'

Dalliances with A-list stars were just all in a day's work for McFly now. In July they flew to Japan to headline Live 8, and their number ones were still coming thick and fast – 'All About You' in March and 'I'll Be OK' in August. And, even despite the darker tones of *Wonderland*, their second album, it still reached the top spot – just in time to launch its accompanying arena tour – McFly's first – which began on 15 September 2005.

I didn't shag her, but we spent the night and had a fumble

They would be joined on tour by a full orchestra. And Harry had noticed that some of the violinists looked as beautiful as they played. Some – or, rather, one in particular. Izzy Johnston was a stunning brunette who had studied at the Royal College of Music in London. Before the tour started, when the crew were all in Bristol one day, he came over and introduced himself, as Izzy recalled to *Hello!* magazine: 'He gave me a kiss on the cheek and it was absolutely love at first sight. I walked away and said to [my friend], "Something just happened to me." It was powerful, like I'd known him forever.'

It still took them a little while to get together, though. It wasn't until McFly played Cardiff on 11 October, almost a month after the tour began, that they kissed for the first time. Harry said simply to *Hello!*, 'We fell in love. We just had this deep under-standing, like no one in this world knows you better.'

James, meanwhile, was getting to know his new bandmates. It was less than a year since Busted had gone their separate ways, but already he had management, a record label and a brand-new album of songs, this time all written by him with various collaborators.

Son of Dork formed in super-quick time with super-talented musicians, who were found, as per Busted, from adverts placed in the *NME* and the *Stage*. It was a five-piece pop-punk band, perhaps a little rockier than Busted, with Steve Rushton sharing lead vocals with James and playing bass; David Williams sharing rhythm guitar with James and doing backing vocals; Danny Hall on drums; and Chris Leonard as the lead guitarist. The band's name came from – what else? – a film, 'son of dork' being a phrase that's chanted in the 1990 movie *Problem Child*.

James held auditions to find his new bandmates. Literally thousands of people turned up – something he found overwhelming. But he was, after all, one-third of what had just been Britain's biggest group. Prolific as ever, he had four songs written even before the band's line-up was finalised. And he'd also got a great producer on board: Gil Norton, a Grammy-award-winning legend in the industry, who had worked with Foo Fighters, Feeder and many others. James revealed to Virgin Media, 'I played him four songs acoustically and he agreed to do it straightaway.'

And the result was pretty special – another stomping pop-punk album about adolescent life: teenage parties, gorgeous girls and nerdy loser kids. Every song told a story. Every tune had a tale to tell. There was a whole new cast of characters, with 'Eddie's

Song' and 'Holly . . . I'm the One' putting names to the heroes and heroines of James's new music. 'Boyband', a pumping anthemic uptempo track, was a clear retort to all those critics who'd dismissed Busted as nothing more than that, co-written by James with Brendan Brown of Wheatus and 'Teenage Dirtbag' fame, with tongues placed firmly in cheeks. It even name-checked McFly.

Yet it was the debut single, released on 7 November 2005, that was the stand-out track of the album. 'Ticket Outta Loserville' was classic James Bourne, and followed neatly on, from a stylistic point of view, from the final official Busted single, the fast-paced and toe-tapping 'Thunderbirds Are Go'. That was hardly surprising when you factored in that James wrote it just two weeks after Busted split. And he was certainly hoping that the new band were going to be *his* ticket out of Loserville.

It got off to a great start. DeLorean car in the video? Check. *Smash Hits* award for Hot New Talent? Check. Top-three hit? Check. James's thank-you note to his friends Pete and Charlie in the album sleeve notes looked prophetic: 'Thanks for being there at the beginning of this year when my life was crap – we sure turned it around!' McFly were, as ever, supportive of James; the new band thanked them twice over in the sleeve notes, just as James was thanked in *Wonderland*'s acknowledgements, too.

And it wasn't just James who was starting to think about new music: Matt, too, was putting his mind to his next venture. He'd been offered a solo deal with Mercury Records and was casting about for inspiration for his new album, which he would write himself. The experiences that had put him into rehab, and his devastation following Busted's split, were a source – at long last – of something positive. Getting back into the studio, he thought, would be like coming home.

Home for McFly, meanwhile, was changing. Following the *Wonderland* tour, they all moved into Princess Park Manor, the complex they knew so well from staying with James and Matt when the band were starting out. Yet Tom was still feeling out of sorts. Having now lived two full years in the public eye, he'd seen the good and bad side of fame. And, much to his horror, he'd been labelled 'the fat one' in the band, something the other boys, completely good-naturedly, ribbed him about, joking that he was pregnant

> **Much to his horror, he'd been labelled 'the fat one' in the band**

in their *CD:UK* appearances, while Danny would tease him in interviews that only five girls fancied him.

Blue already, Tom found himself spiralling into a darker and darker place. He recalled in *Unsaid Things*, 'I was obsessing about being the fat one in the band. I wanted to lose weight, but rather than going about it the sensible way, I pretty much stopped eating.'

Dougie, however, having now turned eighteen, was consuming more and more – of the wrong things. As he put it in McFly's autobiography, 'I [now] had sufficient cojones to ask people about other substances that might be available . . .' And he didn't hold back.

In this climate, Tom decided that he wanted to move in with Giovanna and started hunting for a new home for the couple to share. He then went on holiday to Florida with his family, and found that the sunshine warmed not only his skin but his spirit, too. He turned the corner from his depressive period and came back fighting fit and ready to begin writing McFly's third album, which would be called *Motion in the Ocean*.

And he got some inspiration for the new album's musical direction from an unexpected source: Matt Willis. Matt, who was getting in the zone for writing his own album, had discovered a power-pop band called Jellyfish. Way back in 1993, they had released an album called *Spilt Milk*. It was zany, summery and kooky, imaginative and full of flights of fancy. It seemed to link back to McFly's debut – those light, bright hits and happy days. It seemed like the next step forward for McFly to Matt's musical ear – a more direct, linear link to *Room on the 3rd Floor* than to *Wonderland*. Matt suggested to Fletch – who was by now managing Matt as a solo artist, as well as Son of Dork and McFly – that the McFly boys check it out.

AllMusic.com reviewed *Spilt Milk* in glowing neon terms that showcased just how on-the-money Matt was with his suggestion:

Dreamy vocal harmonies . . . and crunchy guitars are layered in a manner that evokes the best of the Beatles and the Beach Boys. 'Hush', the lead track, particularly recalls the Beach Boys with its luscious vocal harmonies . . . *Spilt Milk* is a flawless pop gem from start right through the unbridled optimism of the closing 'Brighter Day'.

And it was a brighter day indeed for McFly. Inspired by Matt's tip, they set up a home recording studio at Princess Park Manor, and over the course of a week and a half created the magic that

was to become their third album. Has a single block of apartments ever been the scene of such extraordinary music history
before? In the same building where James and Tom had started
their writing partnership, where McFly's debut album and
Busted's second had come together, McFly now proved that lightning definitely strikes in the same place twice.

Meanwhile, James and Tom were still cherishing their unique
writing partnership. Together, they wrote 'Lonely', which would
appear on *Motion in the Ocean*. A typically upbeat and deceptively
simple guitar track, despite the downbeat topic, it was rippled
with McFly's usual harmonies and backing vocals. James also
wrote 'We Are the Young' with Tom and Danny. As Tom put it in
his thank-yous in the album's sleeve notes, 'James Bourne, thanks
for another couple of big fish on this album.' And the duo also
wrote a new song for James's band, 'We're Not Alone', which was
due to be released as the lead single of the deluxe edition of Son
of Dork's album *Welcome to Loserville* in April.

But all was not well in the land of Dork. James confided to The
Vault, 'We released the first song ["Ticket Outta Loserville"]. I
think it was a hit. It came out against
Madonna. It was the second highest
new entry; it was number three. But
everyone was like, "Well, it wasn't
number one so, er, so ..."' And here
James made a slicing gesture across his
throat. He continued, 'I was very happy

But all was not well in the land of Dork

with the number-three result. I felt we were onto something. I
wanted to celebrate when it got to number three. But everyone
around me was saying, "But we don't really celebrate that much

when you get to number one any more, so why would we celebrate when you get number three?"'

When Busted's debut single had been released, back in
September 2002, it had charted at number three – just like 'Ticket
Outta Loserville'. Yet people seemed to think that a top-three hit
now was James failing; that he was on a one-way ticket straight
back to Loserville himself. Later, James would say pragmatically,
'You don't get that many chances. If they feel that you're not
going to get number ones any more after you've had a long string
of number ones . . .' He petered out, but the meaning was clear.

'Eddie's Song', the second single, charted at number ten in
January 2006. Two top-ten hits! It was more than most bands
achieved. But it wasn't enough. With the album peaking at only
number thirty-five and the faith lost, Son of Dork were quietly
dropped from their record label. James and Tom's 'We're Not
Alone' was never released, though it did appear in the Ant and
Dec movie *Alien Autopsy* later that spring.

James's band tried to pick up the pieces, deciding to go it alone
on James's own record label, which he called Sic Puppy, after the
first band he'd formed back in Southend-on-Sea. It was a name
that resonated with him; during the peak of Busted's fame, he'd
set up a skater-style clothing line with the same name. And while
Son of Dork plugged away, doing gigs and setting up a tour with
Wheatus for the following spring, Matt was plugging his guitar
into the amps in the recording studio, overseen by a new producer
by the name of Jason Perry.

Perry was a singer himself, with the band A, and he had a
unique approach to producing. As he said to the magazine *Sound
on Sound*, 'I used to be a singer in a band and I've worked with all

these great producers throughout the years, and the main thing I've learned is I hate vocal booths . . . So my main thing is, let's all just get in a room and do it . . . My main thing as a producer is to get a performance that's believable and energetic and confident.'

Confidence was certainly something that James Bourne had in his former bandmate's solo career. Speaking to the *Birmingham Mail*, James said, 'He's gonna do well because he has good songs. I'm a lot more into Matt's stuff than I am into Charlie's stuff. Matt has such an amazing personality as well. He's a top bloke, very kind-hearted.'

And Matt had poured that kind heart of his into every song on his debut solo album. Unashamedly autobiographical, the tracks on *Don't Let It Go to Waste* shine a light into his thoughts on the Busted split, his struggles in rehab – and his overwhelming love for Emma. Halfway through the album, in contrast to the howling electric guitars and booming rock tracks elsewhere on the record, simple, unfussy chords are played on an acoustic guitar. The song is 'From Myself Baby' and it is an open love letter to Emma Griffiths, a tribute to the support she gave him before and during rehab. She is his saviour. With the backing instruments low in the mix – a violin, some understated percussion – it is an unassuming yet beautiful track, with a humble Matt simply seeking salvation from the woman he loves. A few years before, he'd written in *Busted* that what he wanted in a woman was someone 'who can tell me when I'm letting myself down but do so without nagging me'. In Emma, who'd supported him through rehab, and with whom he had a close, honest relationship, he'd found his perfect match.

Despite the beauty of 'From Myself Baby', the first song to be released from the album would be the rocky 'Up All Night', co-written with Jason Perry and Julian Emery (who also co-produced the album), and released on 22 May 2006. Described as 'furiously danceable' by the BBC and 'pyrotechnic pop to pogo to' by Sing365.com, it was a stadium-rock-style song that shot straight into the top ten, charting at number seven.

As the summer of 2006 really kicked in, Matt found himself back on the promotional merry-go-round, appearing at the T4 on the Beach pop concert in Weston-super-Mare on 18 June. And who should be sharing the bill with him? Only his old friends McFly. As Tom confessed to T4 after the event, when they appeared to promote their new single 'Please, Please' (which just happened to name-check a young woman called Lindsay), it was one to remember.

'Dougie nearly got taken away in an ambulance after that,' he said to presenter Miquita Oliver.

'I threw up,' admitted Dougie.

'Because you were having so much fun?' Miquita asked, a little tongue-in-cheek.

> **Dougie nearly got taken away in an ambulance after that**

Dougie looked sheepish and yet amused at the same time. 'Er … yeah,' he said, with all the shy awkwardness that he'd used to display in the corridors of Gable Hall.

But it was Matt who very publicly ended up having too much fun that summer. Come July, he was back in rehab; this time, to tackle his addiction to cannabis. He later told the *Sun*, 'I began [smoking dope] when I was thirteen and by the time Busted made it big I was accustomed to it. I smoked it every single day. It was a way of life.

'You become immune to its effects, or at least you think you do, when suddenly you find yourself turning a bit weird. If I smoked, I'd become paranoid and forget everything. My memory was shot to pieces. I had no confidence. I always felt I was bad with people, but it was because I was always stoned.'

And it was Emma, once again, who persuaded him to get help. Matt revealed, 'She told me if I had another joint she would leave me. I realised I needed to do something and when she threatened to never speak to me again I took action. Emma was the one who helped me kick my addiction and I will be forever grateful.'

'From Myself Baby' was even more poignant after that. And, fresh out of rehab, Matt released his second single, 'Hey Kid', which charted at number eleven. It was all about the days after Busted split, with a more mature Matt talking to his younger self and counselling him that the band being over didn't mean the end of him. Matt revealed to Sing365.com, '"Hey Kid" is about the week Busted split up ... That night in the hotel [on 14 January 2005], I turned on Sky News and there was the press conference. And we weren't actually shit, we were one of the good ones, I thought. I was always very proud of what we did.'

It seemed he could be proud of his latest hit, too. Sing365.com described 'Hey Kid' with vibrant enthusiasm as 'the biggest anthem Def Leppard never wrote'. Out of rehab and releasing new music, Matt reassured fans all was well, saying to the *Mirror*, 'I'm doing fine. I feel great.' Then he added, almost as an afterthought, 'For now.'

McFly were certainly doing great. Having been inspired by the Jellyfish album Matt had suggested they check out, they now took another tip from him, by booking Jason Perry and Julian Emery to produce *Motion in the Ocean*. No wonder their thank-you to their old friend was so generous in the sleeve notes of the album: 'Matt Willis, we wouldn't be here today without all your help in the beginning. We hope you like this album as much as we all love yours!' And to record the album McFly decamped to the isolated Grouse Lodge in County Westmeath in Ireland – a studio Matt had also used for his solo work – for a recording session that completely revamped how the band worked.

Producer Jason Perry told *Sound on Sound*, 'When I first met the boys ... they always seemed a bit insecure and almost apologetic about themselves. I was like, "You're one of the best bands in the country." I don't think people realise they write the songs and actually play them. You go and see them live and it's like, "Wow, they're amazing."'

And, with Tom in particular, he brought the insecure singer much more confidence. Perry said, 'I remember when I first started working with them, their management pulled me aside and said that Tom loses his voice easily and he's not allowed to eat chocolate. And I was like, "He can do what he wants, he can go and start smoking if he wants. The reason he's losing his voice is he's worried about it." He'll never lose his voice again when I'm around.'

It's a time Tom remembered all too well. 'I got into this habit,' he said to *Sound on Sound*, 'I think under pressure and stress, any morning I knew we were going in to do vocals, I'd wake up with a psychological cold ... I think it was just worrying about it too much. Jason wanted to get away from that ... and it's just really relaxed ... That's the way we ended up getting the best vocally out of me and Danny.'

Tom and Giovanna Fletcher – childhood sweethearts and still going strong.

James with his childhood sweetheart, actress Kara Tointon. Their romantic relationship ended in 2004, but the pair remain friends.

Her frog prince: TV presenter Emma Griffiths met her perfect match in Matt Willis.

Cavorting on the red carpet – but behind the smiles, Matt was struggling with addiction. Emma would be the one carrying him through the tough times to come.

Me and Mrs Jones:
Danny and Georgia Horsley tied the
knot in August 2014.

Harry and Izzy Judd. They met on
McFly's *Wonderland* tour and married
in a magical winter wedding in
December 2012.

Love at last: Dougie and singer
Ellie Goulding.

Wasn't meant to be: Dougie and his
former girlfriend Frankie Sandford
from the Saturdays.

And *Motion in the Ocean* was an album that showed the guys really were back at their best – so much so that Tom, in his sleeve notes, would say to Fletch and Rashman, 'Thank you so much for not putting me in Busted!' Speaking to *Digital Spy*, the band said, '[*Motion in the Ocean*] was a bit of a reaction to *Wonderland*. We made the record in our new flat and produced our own demos. We didn't leave the house for a week and a half and wrote the whole thing. We intentionally wanted to do stuff that was more fun and poppy. There was also quite a strong Queen influence throughout it.'

And Dougie revealed the story behind the name of the album, saying cheekily, 'The title came from someone telling us about their small dick. He said, "It's not the size of your boat, it's the motion in the ocean."'

The album was an unashamedly, gloriously buoyant record, packed with poppy hits – and there were clear chart-toppers among them. Even the 'serious' music press gave the album good reviews, with credible muso website MusicOMH.com celebrating it as 'delightfully undemanding bubblegum pop'. The rave review continued, 'The morose faces of *Wonderland*'s cover are replaced with images of some kerrazy shenanigans involving swimming underwater – wait for it – fully clothed! ... They've rediscovered their sense of fun ... Like candy floss for the ears, there's little substance but it sounds great – brilliantly executed and something you should *not* feel guilty about liking.'

Guilt seemed to be a theme for reviewers, with the *Guardian* writing, 'This third album shows why [McFly still have an audience]: they produce guitar pop of a standard that would have been a credit to the young Supergrass, and refuse to patronise their audience with pallid love songs ... Enjoy without guilt.'

It seemed guilt-free pop was in vogue. As the year drew to a close, McFly were still riding high, with their singles still going straight to number one, including the intergalactical star maker that was 'Star Girl'. Written by the band with Jason Perry, Julian Emery and Daniel P. Carter, the song started out as one they were calling 'Jelly Belly', which had a ridiculous lyric. Then, one night during their Irish recording sessions, Tom had a dream. He dreamed that they'd written a song about falling head over heels in love with an alien. Dougie suggested they try to write that song to the tune of 'Jelly Belly' – and the rest is pop history. The song sold almost 60,000 copies in its first week on sale, proving that McFly really were out of this world.

The boys filmed one of the most fun promo videos ever to accompany the song's release: one of the most fun – and the most hilarious. It starts with Danny looking into a home camcorder, with a fuzzy, almost out-of-focus lens picking out his shaggy dark hair, and a 2006 date time-stamped in the corner.

'Hello, and welcome to Bolton, 2006. It's in my back yard. We've been building a rocket. We're going to send Dougie up into space. Dougie, how d'you feel about going up today?'

'I feel really scared and I think I need more training.'

Cue song. And cue Dougie's 'training': a series of home videos of the boys 'training' him for space travel, which necessitate the slogan 'No Dougies were hurt making this video'. Danny holds up handwritten signs introducing each trial. The 'Re-Entry Test'. The 'Endurance Test'. And the 'G-Force Test', in which Dougie sits in a shopping trolley in a blue jumpsuit and a crash helmet, with a rope attached to his ride, and is flung in steadily faster circles by the boys until he is actually flying through the air at high speed. Interspersed with all these high jinks is footage of the guys playing a live gig – and they look as though they're having just as much fun onstage as they are messing about in Danny's back garden. When your best friends are your bandmates, that does tend to happen. And they were now neighbours as well: when Tom showed the others the house he'd found to buy with Giovanna, all three of his bandmates bought nearby properties.

In November, their new album charted in the top ten, at number six. Sixty places behind them that month was Matt's debut, *Don't Let It Go to Waste*. His solo effort had received incredible reviews: Sing365.com wrote that it was 'a full-on, balls-out monster of a record, with a sound that Matt accurately describes as "stadium pop" – think Robbie, Green Day and Van Halen jamming underneath a firework display . . . The album is simply an awesomely confident record that will make Matt Willis one of the defining stars of 2006 and beyond.' But it seemed that music-buyers hadn't got the memo.

Yet Matt had a master plan – one he would later describe to The Vault as 'one of the most bizarre choices I've made in my life'. He was heading into the jungle as a contestant on ITV's reality show *I'm a Celebrity . . . Get Me Out of Here!*

The papers were full of gossip that James, forever all about the music, didn't support his ex-bandmate's decision to join a lame reality TV show. The *Mirror* quoted an anonymous source as saying, 'James genuinely cares for his mate. He thinks that Matt hanging out with a bunch of nobodies eating bugs will do nothing for his career and destroy all the hard work that he has put into his music since leaving Busted.' The *Metro* said James thought it was 'career suicide'. Meanwhile the 'source' continued to the

Mirror, 'The pair are at loggerheads over this and are barely speaking. Matt thinks James is being a bit of a snob with his high-and-mighty attitude and can't see what the problem is.

'Matt has told him he's not in it for the money as he's giving his £60,000 fee to charity, but sees it as a chance to boost his profile.'

And James couldn't really argue with that. *I'm a Celebrity* was one of the most-watched programmes in the country, regularly pulling in 9 million viewers. Matt would be flown to the Australian jungle to spend nineteen days – if he lasted that long – in the heat and humidity of the rainforest, camping out among the creepy-crawlies with eleven other people of varying levels of celebrity. And it was something even he, with his carefree, devil-may-care attitude, was apprehensive about. 'I was scared about it,' he admitted to EDP24.com. 'I was thinking, "I'm pretty sure I'm not a dick, but how do I know? Maybe people will think I am."'

> **The pair are at loggerheads over this and are barely speaking. Matt thinks James is being a bit of a snob**

And it hadn't been an easy decision. He said, 'Well, you know, they asked me and I said no – I said no four times. Then I thought, "I've got an album coming out, what can I do to raise the game?" I didn't really want to do a reality show, but then I thought, "You only live once." I want to get people buying my records.'

And, with that in mind, Matt found himself bungee-jumping out of a helicopter into the empty abyss of a bright-blue sky.

NINE

Sound of America

The table was lined with wooden platters, topped with smart wooden cloches that concealed the delicacies within. If Matt Willis tried very, very hard, he could maybe kid himself that the long dining table was the centrepiece of a high-class restaurant, and that the two figures standing beside him, attending to his every need, were the smartest *maîtres d'hôtel* London had to offer.

'Something a bit new for you to try,' said *I'm a Celebrity* presenter Declan Donnelly, bending over to lift the cloche from the latest platter. 'Kangaroo anus.'

No, thought Matt, he *definitely* wasn't in London.

It was the eighteenth day in the jungle. Matt was – against all the odds – down to the last three contestants, along with Australian singer Jason Donovan and former Hear'Say member Myleene Klass. The Molesey boy, who by his own admission had 'never been in a forest, let alone a jungle', had survived the bungee jump, three Bushtucker Trials – and separation from Emma. She had watched his progress from afar and told GMTV, 'He was very, very quiet in the beginning. I think it was a bit of a culture shock for him. I think he's just gone, "You know what, I'm here and I'm going to enjoy it."'

Now he had the difficult job of 'enjoying' kangaroo anus. He'd already eaten the live mealworms ('they taste like pus'), the live witchetty grubs (whose innards ran in dark dribbles down his chin) and crocodile eyes. Now he had anus to eat – and crocodile penis to follow. He said with horror to Ant and Dec, 'Everyone's going to talk to me about this – "You ate penis, you ate anus."'

Everyone's going to talk to me about this – 'You ate penis, you ate anus'

Then, with typical Matt spirit, he declared, 'OK, f**k it.' The anus was hard-going – chewier than a car tyre – but the penis, once bitten off at the base, seemed to go down more easily. Ant and Dec, their respect written clearly on their faces, gave him a cold beer to wash down the bushtucker grub. Matt, taking it and heading back to camp, complained, albeit with a wry smile, 'I've got kangaroo anus in my teeth; really good look.'

But what I'm a Celebrity was doing for him was, in fact, to allow the public to get a really good look at the real Matt Willis. His girlfriend Emma said to GMTV, 'People think he's this crazy person who was in a boy band and wants to try and be a rock star, and he drinks a lot and this, that and the other, but he's just the sweetest, most lovely person and so selfless. He's just brilliant, and I'm so pleased people are starting to see that.'

People were – and they loved what they saw. His humour: dressed in an inflatable sumo suit, he looked down at himself and deadpanned, 'And people said, "Matt, don't go on this show, you'll look silly."' His friendly and fun nature: shot after shot showed him laughing and clowning with his campmates, who became true friends (especially David Gest, whose hair Matt would, inexplicably, regularly brush). And, perhaps most of all, his clear love for Emma. The eagle-eye cameras picked up odd hand gestures Matt was doing that became clear were a message to his girlfriend back home; a private joke they had that meant 'I love you.' Matt openly talked about how Emma had changed his life, how she'd put things into perspective for him and how much he totally and utterly adored her. In return, she confided to GMTV, 'It's really emotional. The worst thing is you want to say it back and have a bit of communication and say, "I'm just the same as you, it's mutual!" But you just can't. There's no way of getting in touch with him.'

There wasn't – until the show was over. On Friday, 1 December 2006, Day 19 in the celebrity jungle, Ant and Dec prepared to announce the results. Matt was the underdog going into the final, and not backed by the bookies: there were odds of only 8–1 that he would triumph over the nostalgia for Jason and the all-powerful appeal of Myleene's white bikini. But Matt managed it. He was crowned the King of the Jungle – to his utter amazement.

'This is just weird,' he told Ant and Dec. 'I didn't come in it to win it. I came in it because I've got an album out!'

As he crossed the famous bridge to exit the jungle, fireworks exploding behind him and a wooden sceptre clasped in his hand, Emma rushed through the blinding lights of the photographers'

Emma, I love you 'ever so' much! I would not be here if it wasn't for you

flashes to leap into Matt's arms. She kissed him and kissed him and kissed him, covering his head with kisses as he laughed and squeezed her back. Paparazzi shots had often shown them clowning around together, with Matt giving Emma piggybacks on the red carpet of various events – and here, too, they couldn't help but show their enormous love and pride in one another. Matt had written in his album sleeve notes, 'Emma, I love you "ever so" much! I would not be here if it wasn't for you. Thank you for loving me.' The fact that she loved him back in equal measure was crystal clear as she welcomed home her boy, who had triumphed to be crowned the nation's favourite campmate.

And it looked as if Matt's master plan had worked. His celebrity appearance certainly made more reviewers take note of his album. Critic Jenni Cole on MusicOMH.com had this to say:

Time for a confession here. This has been a slow music week. So in a belligerent, defender-of-the-indie-flame mood, I decide that for a laugh I'll take the new Matt Willis album and give the abandoned little boy-band munchkin a kicking . . . It'll stop me having to watch him stuff his face with maggots as he clutches at reality TV to keep his career afloat.

I don't even plan to give it the full attention I'd usually afford review copies. Instead, I stick it on in the background . . . But then I notice that, actually, I'm tapping my foot. Then I stop emailing and I start to listen. Really listen. And you know what?

Matt Willis's new album is really good. Really, really good. And not even in a poptastic boy-band way. Good in a quite grown-up, rockier than Radio 2 and Heart FM kind of way. His voice has a gravelly quality that defies his age ... [The songs] demonstrate that not only does Willis have a pretty interesting voice, he's actually a decent songwriter as well ...

All of this is very disturbing, because surely the dog ends of Busted that Charlie has flung aside shouldn't be turning out really, really good records? ... It doesn't make sense but then, back in the day, who ever thought that Robbie Williams would turn out to be the most talented member of Take That? Go Matt – I'm sorry I doubted you.

And Robbie Williams was actually rather an apt association. The BBC, too, commented on it, saying that Matt had 'started making waves musically, with pop pundits crawling over themselves to call him "the new Robbie Williams" ... And with his cheeky smile and "I'd like to be his mate" appeal, it's not a bad comparison.'

Yet Matt himself wasn't wholly sold on the idea. He said to EDP24.com, 'I never wanted to be solo. You hear a lot of people saying, "I dreamed about this," but I always wanted to be in a band. I'm still not sure whether I want to be solo. I might go off and try different things. I haven't got a plan.'

Perhaps it was just as well that 'Don't Let It Go to Waste', the third single from the album, charted at only number nineteen. For a start, Matt's 'different things' started happening sooner than he thought they might. On Valentine's Day 2007 he was asked to co-present coverage of the BRIT Awards for ITV2. Three years on from winning two BRITs himself, he was behind the microphone to ask others how it felt to do it. And his relaxed, funny vibe proved so successful with viewers that Matt soon found himself inundated with other presenting offers.

With his album never rising above its desultory chart position of number sixty-six, despite the stellar reviews, Matt the musician started taking a backseat to Matt the TV presenter. And he found it was something he could keep in the family: he and Emma started getting lots of joint presenting gigs together. TV bosses had seen their chemistry and it was just as electric onscreen as off. A host of jobs presenting for MTV, E! and ITV2 followed for the loved-up couple, including presenting the spin-off sister show for *I'm a Celebrity*, which they hosted for two years running.

McFly, too, were still keeping their hand in on the TV front. In June 2007 Dougie and Tom were in geek heaven when the band appeared as themselves in an episode of *Doctor Who*: 'The Sound of the Drums'. And the band also had their own MTV show, *Up Close and Personal*, which followed them on their tour of the same name throughout 2007, with the band sharing behind-the-scenes stories and memories.

Tom was excited, saying, 'I'm going to be crowd surfing at some point with Dougie. I've done it once before, and I didn't jump in: I got pulled in. They rolled me over onto my back and I was on top of them, and then Dougie bombed over me, went straight over . . . and knocked out a load of girls. Dangerous. It's dangerous being in a band. It's one of the most dangerous professions.'

And 'dangerous' professions aren't for everyone. On 11 July 2007, David Williams, Son of Dork's rhythm guitarist, posted on the group's MySpace page that the band had split – something that was quickly denied by James and the other members of the group. David left the band but they were continuing. Lead vocalist Steve Rushton told FleckingRecords.co.uk, 'We are going to carry on as a four-piece. I know Son of Dork can carry on without him.'

But, as Oscar Wilde might have put it, to lose one band member may be regarded as a misfortune; to lose two looks like carelessness. In October 2007, Chris Leonard also left the group, reportedly saying, 'I've left, but to be honest there wasn't really anything to leave. The band wasn't doing anything at all ... So I moved on and I'm making new music.' He would later go on to write a little tune called 'Lego House' with an up-and-coming artist called Ed Sheeran.

For James, it was the second band in less than three years that had fallen apart around him. The band had been performing – they'd headlined the Sic Tour at the Shepherd's Bush Empire back in March, which gave unsigned bands a chance to perform to the public, all hosted by James's old friend Matt Willis – but the momentum had gone out of it. Son of Dork lay in tatters. And James was fed up with the UK, too. As he said to Fearne Cotton on

People here look at you like your career's over

Fearne and McBusted, 'People here, once you've been in a band that's been successful and then it's finished, they look at you like your career's over.'

With Chris's words ringing in his ears, he made a decision. He was moving to America.

New start.

New York.

Manhattan's Lower East Side has always offered a home to immigrants. At 154 Ludlow Street, between Stanton Street and Rivington, lies a red-brick tenement building, where there used to be a little bar on the ground floor called The Living Room. One cloudy November day in 2007, James Bourne pushed his way through its bright orange door and headed inside. He had his acoustic guitar on his back, and a host of songs in his head.

That night, on the little stage, no more than two metres deep and strung with fairy lights, he played a humble acoustic set to a small crowd – his first ever solo gig. Dressed in a simple grey T-shirt with the slogan TOM PETTY, in tribute to the American rock singer, he ran through such hits as 'Crash and Burn' and Son of Dork's 'Sick', as well as trying out '28,000 Friends', a song so new he had to pause before singing it to remember the words. He performed the clearly autobiographical 'What Happened to Your Band?' to powerful effect. He did his own 'echo' special FX (singing while moving his head slowly away from the mic, something that got an appreciative chuckle from the audience). He checked casually with the organiser how much time he had left for his slot – ah, time for just one more.

He asked the crowd if they were having a good time, and the emphatic response declared they truly were. The UK might have made James feel like a failure, but here, on the stage where acts such as Norah Jones had honed their craft, he was simply a very, very good singer-songwriter plying his trade. The *New York Press* had described The Living Room as a place where 'there's still a reverence for the simple quiet tune. Everyone always puts music first and they care so much about the people that play here.' America had just found a new talent to take to her heart.

And there was someone special there watching over James, too. Her name was Gabriela Arciero. She was a gorgeous American girl for whom, just like James, music was everything. On the website of her band Avenue B, a group she later formed with her sisters, she is described as 'the lovable funny one. Her rhythm beats the rest of us so she plays drums and percussion and sings killer harmonies.' It was the perfect match. She and James had met the year before; the fact that his move to America would put him nearer to this woman he thought was wonderful wasn't exactly offputting to him. As he settled into his new American life, moving between LA and New York and occasionally visiting people back in the UK, they grew closer and closer together.

As for the boys in McFly, they were the closest they'd ever been. And, as 2007 drew to a close, they made a decision to stick together, come hell or high water – with or without a record deal. The year had been a turbulent one for the boys. Against their wishes, the record label had insisted on releasing a 'Greatest Hits' album (with accompanying tour) in November. Tom said to the *Guardian*, 'We wanted to make a new album, but there was nothing we could do to stop them.' The album went platinum, but that wasn't the point. As Tom put it to the *Daily Mail*, 'The label released a greatest hits album. We didn't want to do that – it's what you do after ten years.'

McFly had been together for only four. But now, drawing on the close friendships they'd developed in those four years, and their belief in the band, they were flying solo from a big label and setting up on their own. An exclusive *Daily Mail* interview with the band set the scene: 'Some months ago in the London offices of Island Records, a group of twenty-something musicians stood in front of a roomful of experienced music executives and insisted on being released from the multi-million-pound deal that had made them famous.' Danny explained to *Sound on Sound*, 'There was just a creative difference thing. We felt like we were more in touch with the fans than this guy just sat in the office. We left on good terms and they understood why we were doing it. We just said, "Yeah, let's try it on our own."'

And that was exactly what they did. Tom, Danny, Dougie and Harry set up Super Records to release their next album. Harry said to the *Mail*, 'The whole point of setting up our company and doing this new album is that we're going in a new direction – we're growing, we're changing and it's really exciting.' They certainly relished the freedom they now had at their fingertips, as they prepared to record their fourth studio LP, which would become known as *Radio:ACTIVE*. First, they headed to Barbados, although that ended up being more of a party vacation – with some partying harder than others, as Dougie found to his cost when he drank so much that he ended up wetting the bed.

Now twenty, Dougie was starting to become concerned about how often he was getting wasted on drink and drugs. He said in *Unsaid Things*, 'I told myself I was loving this way of life, but I wasn't being honest. I had started to feel – and this is the only way

I can describe it – uncomfortable in my own skin . . . It dawned on me that I wasn't really enjoying what I was doing, but I didn't seem to be able to stop.'

He didn't talk to his bandmates about it. It was his little secret, one he kept as close to him as that skin he so hated. And little Dougie Poynter was such a good actor, so good at covering his tracks, that they didn't have a clue. When they came to promote the new album, Tom would say confidently to the *Daily Mail*, 'None of us do

> **He didn't talk to his bandmates about it. It was his little secret**

drugs,' and Danny would add strongly, 'Why would you want to get into drugs and become a hopeless excuse for a human being?' Dougie had lied about his age to get into the band. Now he found himself lying to stay in it.

From a musical perspective, though, McFly were stronger than ever. In the end, taking producer Jason Perry with them, they decamped to Australia for several months from January 2008 to record *Radio:ACTIVE*. And, with them footing the bill rather than the record label, things were a bit more low-key, as Jason told *Sound on Sound*. 'It was just this grotty little rehearsal place. We had all the gear set up and you could barely get in there. Everyone's just facing each other and it's hot and sweaty . . . We were really working on getting the songs amazing.'

Lizard fan Dougie, an aficionado of all creatures great and small, was in his element. He enthused, 'It was an absolutely tiny room with dodgy Australian spiders in there and stuff.' And

Harry, an Uppingham boy at heart, commented, 'It wasn't what we were used to.' Yet the drummer concluded, 'But it was all we really needed. Just a room.'

Just a room in which to do what they did best. As Danny put it to *Sound on Sound*, 'We literally just made music we wanted to make and produced it how we wanted to produce it. This album's not had any opinions forced on it apart from ours.'

While McFly were relishing the opportunity to make their own music, James and Matt received some unwelcome news relating to theirs – in the form of a summons to the High Court in London.

In the long-ago spring and summer of 2001, when Matt and James would get together at James's house in Southend-on-Sea and at the InterContinental, in the very, very early days of the band, they weren't always alone. Owen Doyle and Ki Fitzgerald had been there, as part of the Termites. Now, their former bandmates took Matt and James to court over ownership of the songs that were written when Busted – in their original line-up – were just starting out.

Rashman had negotiated a split of the songs written in that time, in the formal agreement that Ki and Owen had signed on 22 March 2002. Ki and Owen got 100 per cent of two of the songs – one of which was 'She Knows', in which Sony had expressed keen interest when the band had gone in for their meeting with the executives there, just after they'd signed their management deal with Rashman – and the other four went wholly to James and Matt. They'd all thought it was a done deal, a fair agreement that was negotiated over the course of several months.

But, in 2005, Ki and Owen had lodged a complaint against them, seeking £10 million in unpaid royalties. They said they'd been coerced into signing the agreement that divided the songs up between the four boys, and that 'undue pressure' had been exerted on them to make them sign. On 26 February 2008, the case finally opened at the High Court. The claimants set up a website called whatigotocourtfor.com to champion their cause (the link is no longer active).

James and Matt both appeared to give evidence in their defence, as did Rashman. Fletch gave evidence via video link from Australia, where he was helping McFly to record *Radio:ACTIVE*. Even James's ex-girlfriend Kara Tointon came along to support him; things were good between them. She told the *Mirror* in 2007, 'I've never had a bad break-up . . . I spoke to James Bourne yesterday. He still lives in the same block of flats as me, but he's always in LA so it's not like we bump into each other all the time.' In his hour of need, she was more than willing to show her support.

In presenting his case, Ki took his guitar into the witness box and outlined the songwriting process to the judge, singing Wheatus's 'Teenage Dirtbag' and a version of the Spice Girls' 'Mama' to illustrate his points – something that didn't go down too well with Wheatus's lead singer, Brendan Brown. He told FleckingRecords.co.uk in no uncertain terms, 'On the one hand, it's pure Monty Python genius. You couldn't pay millions to the best video director to paint that picture. Only in this surreal world of ours is that possible [to have my song played in the High Court].

'On the other hand I am a bit angry. I am good friends with

I'll reach down your throat and pull your f**king skeleton out!

James Bourne, I know he was in the right and I thought, "You c**t! How dare you use my song to try and steal from my friend? I'll reach down your throat and pull your f**king skeleton out!"'

While the judge, Mr Justice Morgan, didn't use quite those terms, he did have some pretty damning words regarding Ki's and Owen's reliability as witnesses when he gave his judgement on 6 June 2008. 'Ki was not a reliable and convincing witness,' Morgan began. 'He quite plainly exaggerated and distorted the real events . . . Owen was not a reliable witness, either. He manifested a high degree of confusion and a failure to grasp the detail in relation to many of the significant events.'

The court documents show that Ki and Owen consistently changed their stories. In October 2001, they'd told Rashman that they hadn't contributed to some of the songs. Now, they were claiming co-writer credits.

The judge said of James: 'Conversely, I regard James as an essentially credible and reliable witness. He had a very good and clear recollection of points of detail and the content of his evidence appeared to be credible and was given in a credible way. The only qualification on my assessment of him is that it is possible he was a little ungenerous towards Ki and Owen in describing the contribution that Ki and Owen may have made to the composition of some of the songs. I do not, however, think that he was seriously wrong even in that respect. It is not altogether surprising that his evidence lacked generosity towards Ki and Owen. I think that, towards the end of their relationship in October 2001, it was already the case that James did not altogether like Ki and the way in which the claimants, and in particular Ki, have conducted this litigation ever since would not have done anything to encourage James to look kindly on Ki.'

Matt and James won the case. They issued an uncompromising statement following the verdict:

This was an opportunistic attempt by Doyle and McPhail [Ki's legal surname] to cash in on our success. Their claims were a complete fabrication and we are delighted that the judge has seen through this and totally dismissed them. Our position has been completely vindicated and our achievements with Busted remain untarnished.

The judge chose not to make a pronouncement as to who had written what in relation to the disputed songs. He simply said that the March 2002 agreement that the claimants had signed, in which the fruits of the band were shared out between the four boys, was legally binding – which is, of course, what Rashman had intended it to be when it was first drawn up. Ki and Owen had no claim on the songs they had signed away. After the judgement, they said they would appeal, but no further coverage reports that any such thing took place.

For James and Matt, it had been an extremely tough time, though all James would say on the matter, to FleckingRecords.co.uk, was 'It's not fun, is it?'

Matt expressed himself in his tried-and-tested way. On 6 June

2008, the same day the verdict was returned, it was announced that he had crashed straight back into rehab.

And this time, the papers were full of the story that Emma had given him an ultimatum.

Give up booze – or lose me.

TEN

Only the Strong Survive

Bournemouth on the south coast of England boasts seven miles of golden sandy beaches and a quiet pace of life. Ever since the Queen Mother's ancestor, Mary Eleanor Bowes, escaped there to get away from her violent second husband, it has offered sanctuary and peace to those in need. In the summer of 2008, Matt Willis was just such a person in need.

He attended the Providence Projects rehabilitation centre, a quiet retreat just a short walk from the sandy beaches, to help him battle his drink-and-drug demons once and for

Help came not a moment too soon

all. And help came not a moment too soon. In May, he'd had a wild night out with his old school friend from Sylvia Young, Amy Winehouse – who was herself struggling with her own drug and alcohol addictions – and it was this night, it was reported, that tipped him over the edge. The *Mirror* gave this account: 'Long-suffering Emma was furious when Matt went back to Wino's pad after a night out . . . and even angrier when she saw the state he turned up in at their north London home.'

It was a far cry from the happy time the couple had shared together on holiday in Venice the year before. In March, Matt had whisked Emma away for a romantic weekend – to ask a very special question. Emma told *Bella* magazine, 'Matt went all weird one evening and I thought he was going to finish with me. He wasn't talking and it was really odd.

'We ended up on the Rialto Bridge, which is full of tourists. He kept saying, "Let's go for a walk," but Matt doesn't like sightseeing and I suddenly twigged what was going on.'

Before her disbelieving eyes, Matt took a ring box out of his pocket and opened it up. There was a glittering square-cut diamond ring inside, sprawled somewhat inelegantly on the cushion – a bit like Emma and Matt themselves when one of their red-carpet piggybacks went awry – as it had come unmoored from its fastenings as Matt had nervously walked Venice's streets with Emma, looking for the perfect spot to pop the question. He started to go down on one knee – but his girlfriend stopped him. He rushed out the all-important question and she accepted, immediately. Emma confessed to *Bella*, 'Then I cried and loads of people were looking, which was just embarrassing.

'It was lovely, and I loved that the ring fell out of the cushion and that I wouldn't let him get down on one knee and that he stumbled and that I panicked – that's very us!' She said to the

Mirror, 'We laughed at each other! You feel very grown-up [being engaged]. And a bit daft.'

Matt checked into rehab just weeks before their big day. But, contrary to rumours, he had Emma's support all the way. She told *OK!* magazine, 'It was never a case of, "We're not going to get married [if you don't go to rehab]." It was Matt saying, "I really need to sort my shit out," so he did.'

And, a mere four days before the wedding, he checked himself out of rehab – having completed the full five-week treatment programme. He later said of the experience to *OK!*, 'I knew I had to sort my life out. I didn't want to marry Emma being a liar and hiding things from her. I had been like this for a long while, but as the wedding got closer I remembered I was marrying the girl of my dreams and I didn't want to marry her as a f**k-up. I didn't feel right in my head; I wanted a fresh start. I didn't go in there for a rest. I went to sort my head out.'

Emma later spoke of that time on *Fearne and McBusted*, in an interview that famously reduced her to tears as she recalled Matt's stints in rehab. 'He went to rehab when I'd known him for three months . . . I was in this whirlwind

I didn't want to marry Emma being a liar

with him,' she remembered. 'Then he went again; we'd been together a couple of years. [You realise] this isn't just a kid that needs a couple of weeks' break: it's someone that does genuinely have a problem . . . But I'm not going to leave him because he has a problem. We have to stick together and do it.'

And Matt added, 'It was really tough. It's never easy for anybody. I tried to quit drinking quite a few times. It's a different thing saying, "I think I need to clear myself up a little bit" to actually saying, "I can never do this again. This is a massive problem in my life."'

But with his problems behind him, thanks to the Providence Projects, he now just had the small matter of the biggest day of his life to contend with.

The morning of Saturday, 5 July 2008, saw the sun shining. Blue skies formed a glorious backdrop to the spectacular Rushton Hall in Northamptonshire, where Matt and Emma had chosen to wed. Matt, dressed in a smart black suit with a white tie and buttonhole, waited patiently in the Great Hall for his bride's arrival; she was running late. His hair – as it had been since the demise of Busted – was a very sober, natural brown colour.

Helping the guests to their seats was James, in a grey suit and a white buttonhole to match Matt's, who was acting as an usher. He greeted his ex-girlfriend Kara Tointon, looking stunning in a turquoise-and-black sundress, who was close friends with Matt and Emma too, and doing brilliantly in her career as a leading actress on *EastEnders*. And of course the McFly boys were there as well, back from Australia and the *Radio:ACTIVE* recording. They greeted James warmly; he'd collaborated on more songs with them of late, including 'Everybody Knows' and 'Do Ya', which had made the final cut of the new album.

McFly were suited and booted, too. They all wore dark suits with colourful ties: red for Tom, blue for Danny, purple for Dougie and pink for Harry. But what everyone was really interested in was what the blushing bride was going to wear.

She didn't disappoint. In a full-length gown, Emma walked down the aisle clutching a bouquet of the creamiest blooms, her square diamond engagement ring catching the light as she headed straight for Matt, her eyes fixed only on him. Her dress had a traditional bodice and full skirt, with wide organza straps brushing her shoulders. Her dark hair was swept up and her eyes sparkled.

They exchanged vows before the stone fireplace in the Great Hall. Matt, clean at last and with no secrets from his new wife, simply couldn't stop smiling. When the guests toasted the couple with champagne, he didn't touch a drop.

He didn't need to. The thought of having Emma as his wife was intoxicating enough.

While 22 September of that year didn't mark another marriage, it was a memorable day nonetheless. It was the official release date of McFly's new album, *Radio:ACTIVE* – the first on their own record label. As Tom said in the sleeve notes, 'We've finally made the album we've always wanted.'

Even the artwork looked different. The lyrics – a must-have for fans who wanted to sing along – were handwritten and came complete with doodles and scribblings-out, just as they did in the notebooks Tom used when he was composing. It was the kind of look more usually associated with an artist like Damien Rice. And credible artists were lining up to recommend the band. The *Daily Mail* quoted rock goddess Courtney Love as saying, 'Who says McFly are a boy band? That's insane. Those guys slam.' And Matt Helders of Arctic Monkeys offered, simply, 'You can tell it comes from the heart with McFly.'

And *Radio:ACTIVE* was an album where they were wearing their hearts on their sleeves. Tom enthused in the sleeve notes, 'Making this album has been one of the best experiences of my life. It was truly awesome. I am actually in my favourite band!'

I want to kiss you all!

And Harry offered expansively, 'I want to kiss you all!' The band's happiness leaped off the page – and out of the speakers, too. You could almost hear the fact that Harry was drumming topless and that the songs, at the time of recording, were punctuated with regular ping-pong games between the boys – and Dougie streaking naked through the Australian tropical downpours. Tom said in the band's *The Making of Radio:ACTIVE* documentary that 'we love the way we play live on tour ... We thought: that's the type of record we should make.' And it did have all the energy and fun of a live McFly gig.

Tom added, 'We don't have to put up with a middleman watering down our ideas' – and there was nothing watered down about this album. Danny remembered, 'I'd go to bed [after recording] and my fingers would burn because I'd played so much guitar.' But it was all worth it.

The BBC loved it, saying, 'These boys have broken free and produced a record that is true to themselves and what they've always been about, but with a meatier, punchier sound ... A grown-up move from a newly mature band whose music and lyrics have definitely stepped up a gear, but [whose music] is still just as infectious and smile-inducing as it ever was.' The *Guardian* proclaimed: 'As a declaration of independence, *Radio:ACTIVE* does them proud.'

The band chose to release a special edition of the record free with the *Mail on Sunday* – a move that boosted the paper's circulation by 300,000 copies that week. Tom explained the decision to the BBC: 'We get to put [the album] into almost 3 million homes, which is an incredible opportunity for us. Hopefully, the 3 million people will all enjoy the music and they'll decide to see us when we go on tour.' The album went top ten, as did its first single, 'One for the Radio', which was written by Tom back in Princess Park Manor.

The song's video started with a little scene played out by Danny, which was inspired by a movie. Which movie? Which other movie is there? It was *Back to the Future*, of course. Danny was seen turning up the dials on his amps, plugging in his guitar and preparing to rock out on a white guitar. As he strums the first note, he's blasted backwards by the wave of sound, before the song kicks in.

The single hit number two in November 2010. McFly's bid for freedom was paying off.

And the boys were relishing the freedom to wear whatever they wanted, too. For it seemed the record company had tried to control even their outfits; as Dougie told the *Guardian*: 'Once, around the time we did the Sport Relief single, they decided that, from that point on, only one of us could wear shorts at any one point.' Dougie, who was still rocking a skater-boy look, with printed T-shirts and shorts and bandanas tied around his long blond hair, won out as the shorts wearer of the group, but now the others could join him. Around that time, in fact, they were all rocking a longer-haired look, apart from Harry, who had settled into his natural brown hair colour and looked as hot as ever. The guitarists would flick long waves of sweaty hair out of their eyes as they raced around the stages of their latest tour with irrepressible energy.

And it seemed Dougie's skater-boy look had caught the eye of a special someone. In the autumn, Dougie started dating a young singer called Frankie Sandford, a slim brunette who was part of a new girl group called the Saturdays, who were just starting to rack up top-ten hits of their own. The following year, they announced that they would be releasing a new single, 'Forever Is Over' – written by none other than James Bourne. (He also recorded the guitar riff for the track, which went to number two in the charts.) Frankie's bandmate Mollie King told the *Daily Star*, 'We heard the song playing while at our record company and went into the office, where James was talking to the head of the label. We said: "We have to have that song." Then we found out that Kelly Clarkson was fighting for it, but he gave it to us. James is lovely.'

Dougie's skater-boy look had caught the eye of a special someone

Not only lovely – prolific. James hadn't been idle while he and Gabriela had been living in America. As he put it to FleckingRecords.co.uk, 'What do you think I do with myself every day? Stay in bed? Music is my thing; I'm non-stop in the studio.' He'd found the time to write music, in collaboration with Take That's Gary Barlow, for an ITV teen series called *Britannia High*, which was the brainchild of *Strictly Come Dancing*'s Arlene Phillips and West End producer David Ian, all about a *Fame*-style school. (Perhaps he asked Matt and Tom for advice on what it was like to attend Sylvia Young.) He'd launched a new band, Call Me When I'm 18, with the social-networking site Bebo tagline 'Another day, another band'. Yet, perhaps still burned by his

Busted and Son of Dork experiences, he was also going solo. The new band's Bebo page said, 'James is still going forward with his solo career, but is in this band to pass the boredom.'

In June, James made an announcement about said solo plans. In *Fearne and McBusted*, he commented, 'What was so cool about being [in America] was that people ... saw me as someone who had a future.' He now revealed that all of his solo endeavours would be released under the name Future Boy. You know, that just happens to be the Doc's nickname for Marty McFly in *Back to the Future* too ... James said pointedly to FleckingRecords.co.uk about the enterprise, 'It can't split up, 'cause it's just me.'

He'd also received a new commission: to turn the songs of Son of Dork's album – those teen-life tracks starring Eddie and Holly and the rest – into a full-blown musical, *Loserville*. The songs were so full of storytelling and character that the idea of applying a bigger narrative to them made perfect sense. James was thrilled, saying to FleckingRecords, 'The songs didn't realise their full potential with Son of Dork. I always believed those songs were bigger than what the band became.' At last, he was able to dust off 'We're Not Alone', the song he and Tom had written together for Son of Dork, which had never been released, and include it in the show.

His collaborator for the epic adaptation would be Elliot Davis, a creative with heaps of experience in the West End, who had previously worked on shows such as *Miss Saigon*, *Cats* and *Les Misérables*. It was an obvious fit for James: he and Elliot had known each other for years and years – they used to live in the same building, and had met on the tennis courts of Princess Park Manor way back in the days of Busted – and it was Elliot who had suggested the whole enterprise. They were commissioned by Youth Music Theatre, the UK's leading musical-theatre company for young people; the premiere would be in August that year.

And James was busy writing for other artists, too. Tom said in *Unsaid Things* that, right from the start of Busted, 'James was aware of the amazing opportunity he'd been given to make a career out of his music. He was far more passionate about songwriting than about partying. Maybe that was the reason why he and I had such a great relationship, because I was just the same.' And as a songwriter with an impressive array of top-ten smash hits, James was in demand. As well as the hits with McFly, he penned tracks for Spice Girl Melanie C and Boyzone, and allowed *X Factor* finalist Eoghan Quigg to record '28,000 Friends' – the new song James had debuted at The Living Room – after enjoying his cover of 'Year 3000' on the ITV talent show.

And then came an opportunity that blew his mind. He wrote 'Don't Try This At Home' for the Backstreet Boys. James had always loved the group. Their songs – some written by Max Martin, whom James idolised – were the kind of stand-out pop hits he really admired; ones that Tom Fletcher had studied back when he was learning how to structure songs. And now James had the chance to write for the band. The Backstreet Boys recorded the tune for their 2009 album *This Is Us*; it didn't make the final track listing, but they toured live versions of it. And it was a hit with the fans, with one admirer writing on YouTube, 'When I found that James Bourne had written this song for [BSB] I was so happy. Backstreet Boys and Busted are two of my favourite musical groups of all time. Both bands have been such an inspiration to me. I have no words to explain how great it is that James wrote a song for BSB!!!'

Matt Willis, meanwhile, had been productive in rather a different way. On 20 June 2009, he and Emma welcomed into the world their daughter, Isabelle Catherine Willis. Matt tweeted two days later, 'Isabelle Catherine Willis was born at 9.05 p.m. on Saturday the 20th! She is AMAZING and doing really well! Taking her home today.'

And Matt wasn't the only one settling into domestic bliss. It seemed that McFly's loved-up bandmates had finally rubbed off on Danny. In November it was announced that he'd started dating Miss England 2007, Georgia Horsley, a beautiful blonde from North Yorkshire.

However, their union wasn't without its controversy. Danny's previous girlfriend was Miss England 2008, a fact with which the tabloids had a field day. Danny had once been stung in a tabloid kiss-and-tell at the very start of the band's career, and swapping one Miss England for another seemed straight out of tabloid heaven, too.

Yet this match was clearly meant to be. Danny and Georgia met at the Miss London competition, which was being hosted by the two former Miss Englands, and a friend told the *Sunday Mirror*, 'You could see that Danny and Georgia were going to get together. All the chemistry was there.' Danny himself was clearly smitten, saying on *All Star Mr & Mrs*, 'She's basically my life. She makes me smile every day. And she just makes everything . . . great.' And he confessed in *Unsaid Things*, 'The old Danny, the kid in a sweetie shop every time pretty girls were around, is gone. I don't want anybody else but her.'

Just as Danny was settling down, his bandmate Harry's relationship with Izzy – which had been going strong ever since the *Wonderland* tour – suddenly hit a roadblock. Commitment issues were at the heart of it.

But Harry told the *Daily Record* that, after they'd agreed to split, Izzy turned up on his doorstep one night. It was a night that changed everything. 'She was standing there in tears, with make-up running down her face. I knew then that I couldn't ever be without her.' And Izzy later mused to *Hello!*, 'If you survive difficult times, it just affirms that you want to be together.'

> **She was standing there in tears ... I knew then that I couldn't ever be without her**

While Harry and Izzy took time to focus on their relationship, the rest of the band headed to Atlanta to work on their new album, which would become *Above the Noise*. Record labels had been so keen to work with them after the success of *Radio:ACTIVE* that the band found themselves 'signing on' again. And, as they flew off to start work, they heard some good news. In the spring of 2010, Radio 1 DJ Chris Moyles decided to start a new feature on his super-popular breakfast show. Every Friday, he would play the upbeat 'Star Girl' to kick off people's weekends – dubbing the weekly feature 'McFly Day'. For the 8 million listeners, McFly soon became synonymous with good times, freedom and the start of the weekend. So let the good times roll

And in Atlanta they certainly did. With a big label behind them, the band found themselves in a position to work with the

Partying too hard: in 2005, Matt crashes into rehab. It won't be the last time.

Don't let it go to waste: Matt launches his solo career in 2006.

Ticket Outta Loserville? James's new band, Son of Dork, rock out onstage.

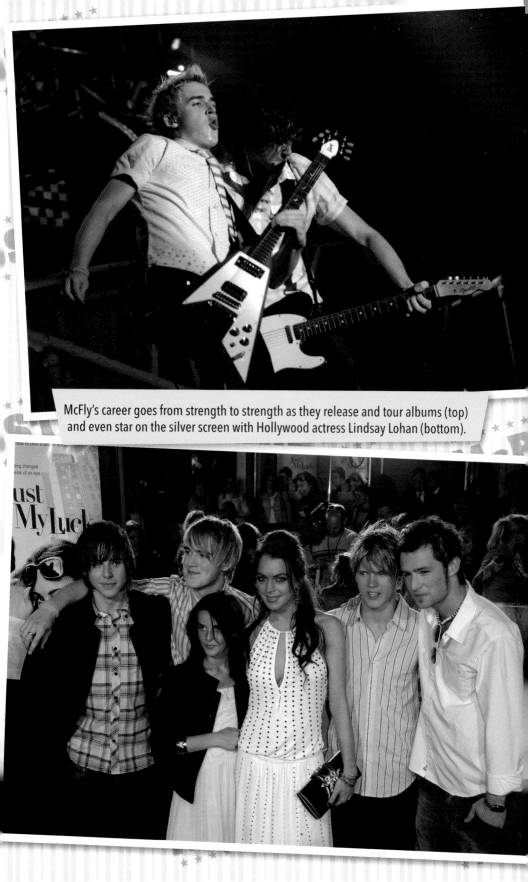

McFly's career goes from strength to strength as they release and tour albums (top) and even star on the silver screen with Hollywood actress Lindsay Lohan (bottom).

What I go to court for: James and Matt defend
themselves against their former bandmates' claims.

Dougie, Danny and Harry show their support at the premiere of James's
new West End musical, *Loserville*, in October 2012.

Reality-TV royalty: Matt is crowned King of the Jungle in 2006 (top); Dougie does it again down under five years later (middle); while Harry and his dance partner Aliona Vilani waltz off with the *Strictly Come Dancing* glitter-ball trophy in 2011 (bottom).

legendary producer Dallas Austin. His clients included Madonna, Pink and Lady Gaga – and Tom and James's old favourite Michael Jackson. It was an opportunity they couldn't pass up.

Yet the making of *Above the Noise* proved to be an experience that differed completely from any album they'd ever done before. As the writing and recording began, staged in the end in both Atlanta and London, across the course of 2010, the band lived a lifestyle that Tom described in *Unsaid Things* as 'totally nocturnal and constantly drunk'. The time in the studio was interspersed with visits to bars and strip joints. Dougie threw himself into the new lifestyle with his usual abandon, until even Tom started noticing something was up. As he said in the band's autobiography: 'I couldn't help noticing that Dougie was acting weird. He would disappear for a while, then come back bouncing off the walls, talking nineteen to the dozen.'

And Dougie had more reason than ever to want to drown his sorrows in booze and narcotics. He and Frankie – who had been dating solidly since 2008 – split up in the spring of 2010. A 'friend' told the *Metro* that, soon after the split, Frankie 'came back in tears and said she made a mistake'. They were back on – for now.

> **The time in the studio was interspersed with visits to bars and strip joints**

There was great interest, meanwhile, in whether there might be a reunion of a different sort in 2010. Matt and James both faced constant questions as to whether Busted might get back together. Matt, who was busy being a stay-at-home dad to little Isabelle, as Emma's presenting career went from strength to strength, revealed to *This Morning* in September 2010, 'Me and James kind of had *the* chat. A shall-we-get-the-band-back-together? kind of chat – but . . . Charlie wouldn't do it, so it'd be me and James and there's questions like, "Do we keep it the two of us? Would we get a brand-new member in?"

'We'd love to do it, don't get me wrong. I loved that band. I have such an affinity for everything we did with that band . . .' Yet with his new family commitments, suddenly life wasn't as simple as it once had been. The carefree lifestyle Matt had used to enjoy, where he was at liberty to join a pop band on a whim and travel the world, didn't gel with now being a dad-of-one and a supportive husband. He confessed that, despite his passion for all things Busted, 'Right now, I couldn't see myself being away from home eight months of the year. I don't know if I'm quite ready to give my life back to that.'

Meanwhile, James had been musing on the situation too – not that he would ever have broached the subject with Charlie himself. He told FleckingRecords.co.uk, 'Matt actually asked Charlie if he would mind us using the name Busted without him. He said no [to use of the name]. We invited him back, knowing he wouldn't be into it. He doesn't want to come back, but he doesn't want me and Matt to do it without him either.' Years after the band had split, they were still banging their heads against the same brick wall.

Matt confirmed the sad situation to the *Daily Record*, confiding that, 'Charlie didn't want to play ball. We tried to buy the name off him but he wasn't willing to sell it. It is not worth the fight.'

There was one good thing that came out of the conversations between the former bandmates, though. James and Matt had always enjoyed writing music together, and they were slowly rediscovering that shared passion, and the special connection the two friends had always had when it came to making music. Matt revealed to *This Morning*, '[Our conversations] got me and James in a room with two acoustic guitars writing songs for another Busted record. Which we did. We wrote about six tracks which are the best we've ever written. And, whether Busted happens or not, there will definitely be something between me and James happening.'

James was still writing his own material, too. In the summer of 2010, he released his debut album as Future Boy. *Volume 1* had a staggered release on James's website, and appeared in two halves: Side A and Side B. The music was completely different from his usual style: electronic, rather than guitar rock. James said explicitly on his website, 'This is not a rock album. This is 100 per cent electronic.'

It was unlike anything he'd done before. The music, an album of ten songs, is an unusual mix (for James) of chilled-out tracks and more upbeat dance music, all with an electro-vibe sound effect on James's voice. Gabriela appeared with him on the song 'Internet', sharing vocals in a futuristic-sounding duet between the two lovers.

And *Above the Noise*, too, turned out to be a very different record for McFly. It was the first to which James contributed no songs. Tom would later tell *Digital Spy* that it was their 'least favourite' album. He continued, 'We thought we'd try something really drastic and try a completely different producer from a different genre of music.' And, while they all said it had been a 'great experience' of which they had 'fond memories', Harry was almost damning of the first single, 'Party Girl': 'It was like a bad version of a Lady Gaga song . . . It really wasn't us.'

What also wasn't him, suddenly, was drinking. Harry gave up alcohol around this time. He said to *Attitude* magazine, 'You know how people get hangover blues? I just started to not cope with them well, anxiety-wise, to the point where I was being really horrible. Drinking was my vice.' Other than that short soundbite, and a comment to the *Daily Record* that he 'only ever used to drink to get drunk', he has never been drawn on exactly what prompted him to become sober, saying only to Fearne Cotton on *Fearne and McBusted*, 'Something happened that definitely changed me a lot. It affected me in a way that was very horrible, frightening. And so I was, like, well, I'm never doing that again.

'I had [a wake-up call] – in a way that no one would want that to happen to them again. It was a blessing in disguise. It meant that I never touched anything ever again.'

But Dougie was about to take his addiction to a whole new level.

In November, he and Frankie split up again. This time it was permanent. She moved out of the north London home they shared, and Dougie was on his own. A friend told the *Metro*, 'Dougie is devastated. He didn't see it coming at all and still doesn't know why.' Dougie himself told *Sugar*, 'I was gutted about the break-up . . . I really thought things were going well between us.'

He would later say they both had their own issues and were 'entirely unsuited'. Frankie would indeed reveal that she had been depressed for years, telling *Glamour* in 2012 that she found herself in a 'spiral of negative thinking – [thinking] that if I disappeared, it wouldn't matter to anyone. In fact, it would make everybody's life easier. I felt that I was worthless, that I was ugly, that I didn't deserve anything.'

Without Frankie around, Dougie found that he didn't have to keep up his pretence any more. He said in *Unsaid Things*, 'You know that feeling of freedom you get when a relationship ends? It was dangerous for me. Now that I didn't have to hide anything from anyone, I could abuse my body in whatever way I saw fit.'

It was a time that McFly called the 'Great Depression'. They were disappointed with *Above the Noise*, from both creative and commercial perspectives. It peaked at number twenty, their worst-performing album by some way. It may have contained the anthemic 'Shine a Light', which reached number four and endured beyond the album, but one song couldn't lift a record that Dougie dubbed 'too generic'. It barely contained a guitar riff. The band also launched their Super City website, a subscription service for fans, amid great to-do, only to see it crash on its first day – to McFly's huge disappointment and embarrassment. Everything seemed to be falling apart.

> **Now that I didn't have to hide anything from anyone, I could abuse my body in whatever way I saw fit**

It was little wonder that Tom, always susceptible to depression, began to feel that black dog barking at his shins once more, then leaping into his lap and settling like a heavy weight around his soul. He and Dougie would share morose late-night drinking sessions in the dark winter nights, glumly marinating in the hopelessness of life.

One night, Dougie said something that crystallised it all.

'Mate, f**k it,' Tom recalled him saying, in *Unsaid Things*. 'Let's just do one more album and then call it quits.'

Tom stared at him.

Was McFly over?

Deep in his heart, it felt like it.

ELEVEN

Nowhere Left to Run

The applause was deafening. Three thousand people hollered and whooped as the cast of *Footloose: The Dance Musical* came onstage for their curtain call at the famous Edinburgh Playhouse on Greenside Place. They were on their feet, singing and dancing along with the toe-tapping music from the classic eighties film.

The footlights nearly blinded Matt Willis as he took his bow, dressed in the black jeans and black T-shirt of his bad-boy character Chuck Cranston. He was part of the spring 2011 UK tour of the stage musical – and he was loving every minute.

He told the Cornish paper the *West Briton*, 'I went to drama school and this is what I trained for. I've been wanting to do a show like this for a long time. This is pure entertainment.' He added cheekily, 'I don't remember the film but my wife loves it; she's a bit older than me.'

And all that training at Sylvia Young had paid off. This was Matt's second musical-theatre role now; he was leaving his presenting days behind him to follow his first love: performing onstage. The previous year, in the autumn, he'd played Nick in *Flashdance: The Musical* in the West End. Matt described that character to the *Liverpool Echo* as 'a really nice guy, almost geeky ... quite like me' – but Chuck was a different matter. Matt said to the *Daily Record*, 'In *Footloose*, I'm in at the deep end. Chuck's a nasty character, he is the trailer-park trash of the town. He hits his girlfriend, although you don't see that onstage.' And, like many actors before him, Matt was discovering that being a bad boy had its benefits. He said to the *Echo*, 'The more I did it, the more I realised that I quite liked being an arrogant dick. Actually this is quite fun!'

> **The more I did it, the more I realised that I quite liked being an arrogant dick**

The dancing was a challenge, though. Matt might have been able to pull off Busted's guitar-thrashing jumps, but a highly choreographed swing routine was a different matter. He said to the *Daily Record*, 'I've never danced in my life and am really struggling. Obviously, I'm not doing anything like the dancers, but I am learning how to move and sing at the same time. I'm throwing myself on my knees, jumping up, catching a girl – and I have to try to breathe and sing. I hope I don't look too ridiculous ... but I'm loving it.'

And the audience in the Edinburgh Playhouse were loving it, too. The cast took one final bow and made their way backstage to their dressing rooms, the applause still ringing in their ears. The Playhouse was notoriously haunted, but Matt wasn't disturbed by spirits of any kind. In fact, he'd laid his old ghosts well and truly to rest.

Emma Willis said to *OK!* magazine after Matt finished rehab, 'To start with I was watching him all the time. The nice thing is now when he comes home I'm pleased to see he's on two feet and can walk in a straight line . . . I think every day he's getting better.' She found it hard being apart while Matt was away on tour, though. She said to *Closer* magazine, 'In one way it's nice because you have that time on your own – the house is a lot tidier! But I do miss him terribly. I'm fine for a couple of weeks, then I have a little breakdown, he reassures me and it's okay again. It's just working at it really.'

For Matt, it wasn't just his relationship with Emma that he worked at. He'd been clean for almost three years. But, when he was asked by FleckingRecords.co.uk if he was 'completely better now', he replied simply, 'I try every day.'

As he changed out of his costume in his dressing room, his phone began to ring. He glanced at the screen, and answered swiftly.

It was Dougie Poynter on the end of the line. And he needed Matt's help very, very badly indeed.

It was a few days earlier. It was 5 a.m. It was a cold February morning, and the sun wouldn't rise for another two hours. In the dark, Dougie walked out of his house. He had a hosepipe clutched in his hand. Determinedly, he pushed it into the exhaust pipe of his Audi Q7 and then looped the other end through the driver's window. He closed the window as much as he could, so that only the nose of the hosepipe snuck into the car's leather interior.

He sat in the driver's seat. He put the keys in the ignition. He started the engine.

Dougie Poynter wanted to die.

Dougie Poynter wanted to die

He couldn't remember the last time he'd been sober. He wanted the drugs and the drink out of his life, but he'd tried and failed so many times before to kick his habits that he knew it was hopeless.

There was no one he could talk to. Who would understand?

There was only one way to end this.

He sat solemnly in his car, inhaling the exhaust fumes as deeply as he could. Surely, any moment now, he'd fall asleep – just like the girl in the song on the *Wonderland* album. Any minute now . . .

But twenty minutes later he was still awake. Still alive. He said in *Unsaid Things*, 'That was my nadir. My lowest point . . . I couldn't even kill myself. I'd tried and failed – like I had with everything else in my life.'

Yet he still had a life. And he knew, now, that he couldn't handle this alone. He went to his doctor, who referred him to a counsellor. He turned up to the appointment lashed on whisky and the counsellor's verdict was instantaneous. Dougie had to go into rehab.

They found a place for him at the Priory. In two days' time, he'd start a rehabilitation programme that would hopefully save his life.

Two days. He had two days to tell Tom and Danny and Harry the secret he'd been keeping from them for years. Two days before he couldn't touch another drop of alcohol ever again. Two dark, dark days.

Danny said on *Fearne and McBusted*, 'He was scared about telling me. Thought I'd tell him off. But it's fine.' His girlfriend Georgia added, 'We didn't have any idea of the scale of it. He masked it so well. It was quite a shock when it all happened.'

The night before he went into rehab was Valentine's Day. Dougie, after his recent split from Frankie, clearly had no plans – something Harry and Izzy suddenly realised. Izzy told *Hello!*, 'We were on our way out to dinner and it felt wrong. We thought, "We can do this another time."' They went straight round to Dougie's instead, with a plan to keep him sober on his last night of freedom.

But, when they got there, Dougie already had a bottle of Jack Daniel's bourbon out, with not much left inside it. Harry and Izzy stayed as late as they could, then called Tom, who lived next door, to help him make it through the night. 'I would do it for any friend,' Harry said of their intervention to *Hello!*. 'He was very vulnerable at that time.'

Tom stayed with Dougie, trying to make him feel positive about the experience to come, and drove him to the Priory the next morning. They pulled up outside the north London centre. They walked up the steps of the yellow-stoned, double-pillared building and through the black front door together. Dougie remained calm as they checked in at the polished wooden reception desk. He was OK as he and Tom settled him into his room. It was pleasant enough: an armchair, a desk, a bed, and a window looking out onto the green lawns that surrounded the centre.

'Then the time came for Tom to leave,' Dougie remembered in *Unsaid Things*. 'For me to be alone without my bandmates to support me. And it was only once he had driven away from my new home that the reality sank in: there wasn't going to be a drink at the end of this day ... It was, beyond question, the most scared I'd ever been.'

And there was only one person he knew who'd managed to face down that fear. Only one person among Dougie's close friends that he knew had once been just as frightened and as scared as he was, sitting in his room at the Priory that February morning.

That person had defeated his demons.

Maybe he could help Dougie to do the same.

Matt and Dougie spoke every day on the phone while Dougie was in rehab. Dougie later said in *Unsaid Things*, 'Just to talk to someone who'd been through it was a relief; just to know that someone else had experienced the same as me and come out the other end gave me the little bit of courage I needed to see it out.'

And his bandmates, as ever, were also with him every step of the way. They visited the Priory regularly and were always on the end of the phone if he needed them. And they were so proud of him when he completed the twenty-eight-day programme. Harry said to *OK!*, 'It was really hard. He's one of my best mates. He was fifteen when he joined the band and I looked after him a lot. I was really upset for him, but he's turned his life around. He's a credit to himself. He's very mature for his age and – like Tom and Danny – he's a very special person and very unique.' Danny added on *Fearne and McBusted*, 'He's proved himself to be a very strong human being.'

And Dougie was proud of himself. He said to Fearne Cotton, 'You don't even realise how bad it is until you stop [taking drugs]. Man, it got really dark. I don't know how much worse it could have gotten. I don't really want to know. I'm thankful [rehab] happened when it did . . . It's the most life-changing thing I think I've ever done. It's the best thing I've ever done.'

And for his fellow bandmate, Tom, going to the doctor was the best thing he'd ever done, too. After Dougie's suggestion in their drunken chat before Christmas that McFly was over, Tom had taken a good hard look at himself and what he wanted – and really examined why, despite all his success, and all the dreams he'd made come true, he was still utterly miserable. Why was he sometimes able to be so creative and happy, and at others too depressed even to get out of bed?

> **When I heard about bipolar, that really struck a chord with me. [I thought,] That is exactly my life. That is exactly what I go through**

He spoke about it to Fearne Cotton on *Fearne and McBusted*. 'The thing that really made me go and get help was hearing about bipolar. I could recognise that . . . my ups and downs went in sync with our life as a band. When I heard about bipolar, that really struck a chord with me. [I thought,] That is exactly my life. That is exactly what I go through.'

He was prescribed medication to treat his condition, and he

and his bandmates noticed an immediate improvement. Gone was the moody Tom, who might snap in rehearsals or be down on ideas. Tom said to Fearne, 'Instantly [the medication helped]. Within the first few weeks. Harry was like, "You've got your laugh back."

'"What do you mean?" [I said.]

'"You haven't laughed like that in four years."'

And with his laugh back, and his depression properly diagnosed, there was one person in particular that Tom wanted to thank. He'd written in the sleeve notes of *Motion in the Ocean*, 'Giovanna, thanks for putting up with me ... Thank you for always making me smile.' He now had a very, very special plan to put the biggest smile in the world on his gorgeous girl's face – and it involved his and Matt's alma mater, the old school building of the Sylvia Young Theatre School, where he and Giovanna had first met all those years ago in assembly when they were just thirteen.

That was over a decade ago now. Sylvia Young had been running her school in the same place for a long time – but, just as Tom prepared to pop the question, he discovered that she had sold the building. It was being renovated and would soon be unrecognisable to its former students. Tom didn't waste a moment. He gained access to the building, which had been stripped back to its original, dramatic church walls. It was a historic venue for a historic event in his life – the perfect setting. He lit atmospheric candles to compliment the imposing architecture, and then pressed play on the music he'd prepared. Giovanna had been lured to the spot by a producer friend of Tom's. And she told the *Mirror*, 'I got there, opened the door and could hear music playing and there were candles all down the stairs. My reaction was to shut the door! I was like, "Oh my God."'

After asking Giovanna to marry him, Tom added to the *Mirror*, 'It was amazing. We both cried. It was emotional – not just for getting engaged, but being in the place where we met, knowing it was the last time we would see it like this.'

Dougie, who'd moved in with the pair since coming out of rehab, was one of the first to congratulate them – in his own special way. As an engagement gift, he gave them novelty salt-and-pepper shakers in the shape of a penis, and a chocolate 'edible anus'. Whether Matt Willis's exploits on *I'm a Celebrity* were the inspiration for the latter was not revealed . . .

With Tom and Dougie back on an even keel, the band were stronger than ever, as they embarked on their first global stadium tour to promote *Above the Noise*, visiting Spain, Asia and South America as well as venues in the UK. They delayed the first few dates due to Dougie's treatment, but, once they were away, nothing could hold them back – although things were a little different backstage to begin with, as Danny told Fearne Cotton. 'At first, we didn't drink in front of [Dougie]; we didn't have drinks in the dressing rooms . . . We did what we felt was right.'

A camera crew followed them on the tour for the brilliantly titled documentary *McFly on the Wall*. And as Dougie giggled with his bandmates, and they all ribbed each other mercilessly and played practical jokes on one another, it seemed the good times were here to stay. After their wobbles before Christmas, the band were back together for good.

James and Matt's attempts at a reunion, however, were still hanging in the balance. Matt said to the *Daily Record*, 'I've been writing with James. It's going really well. I don't know if we are going to shop it to record companies, release it ourselves or go on a little tour, but it's more of a passion project. Theatre is something I am doing career wise, but music never goes away, music is my passion.'

He continued to The Vault, 'I love making music. I write music all the time – which is really annoying as I don't really have an outlet for it. I don't really want other people singing my songs.' And Busted was still his first love; it was where he felt at home. Being a solo artist hadn't been for him: elusive chart success aside, he hadn't felt comfortable without his bandmates around him. Matt was a social creature, with a ready laugh and a quick wit; the lonely spotlight of the solo career didn't suit him. Yet without a group, and without a career in pop music any more, his frustrated ambitions weren't being realised any time soon. Reviving Busted felt like a pipe dream – but it didn't stop him dreaming nonetheless. He explained, 'I want to be back in that band. I love that band . . . I have looked into it. I have thought about it a few times and the thought is still in the back of my head; in fact it's con-stantly there . . . I would genuinely love to play shows as Busted again. James is one of my best pals in the world and we speak to each other really regularly and, if we can sort ourselves out and sort our lives out, maybe we'll do something.'

Reviving Busted felt like a pipe dream

James, too, was keen on the idea, saying to FleckingRecords.co.uk that, 'It's really unlikely I'd do another Son of Dork album. I'd rather work with Matt Willis again.'

But, for all the fans out there who were getting excited, James added to The Vault, 'I would never begrudge the fans a reunion – but I don't believe in us coming back [just the] two of us.'

It was Matt who summed up the result of all their discussions, with a conclusive statement to the *Daily Record*. It was bleak in its finality.

'We'll most probably never do Busted again.'

TWELVE

I'll Be OK

'Please welcome to the dance floor – dancing the cha-cha-cha – Harry Judd and Aliona Vilani!'

The inimitable voice of the *Strictly Come Dancing* announcer, Alan Dedicoat, boomed out in the *Strictly* studio on Saturday, 1 October 2011. As Maroon 5's 'Moves Like Jagger' was played by Dave Arch and his orchestra, Harry executed one of the most nerve-racking things he'd ever done: performing a Latin dance number to 9 million viewers. Having to sing Busted's 'Year 3000' with Danny in his scary McFly audition had nothing on this.

He'd been shaking beforehand, but the dance that he delivered was smooth, focused and more than competent. Head judge Len Goodman said afterwards, 'All the way through I was thinking, Dirty Harry – make my day, punk. Do a good cha-cha-cha. And I tell you what . . . you did!' Alesha Dixon agreed, saying, 'Harry, I think you're wasted behind the drums, you really look at home on the dance floor.'

Tom and Danny were in the studio audience to cheer him on and, along with the rest of the crowd, gave him a standing ovation. Harry said afterwards of his bandmates, 'I hope I did them proud.' Judging by their beaming grins at the camera and the thumbs-up Tom gave him, that was a given.

The opportunity to appear on *Strictly* had come up while McFly were on tour. The band weren't strangers to reality TV shows. As well as seeing their close friend Matt Willis triumph on *I'm a Celebrity*, Harry's girlfriend Izzy had got to the final of Simon Cowell's *Britain's Got Talent* in 2008, with her string quartet Escala. And Danny himself had taken part in the first series of ITV's *Popstar to Operastar* in 2010; the singer who had once said 'Did you hear my voice?' at the end of '5 Colours in Her Hair' showcased just what an incredible voice it was. The boy from Bolton learned traditional Italian opera and performed it confidently week after week in front of his supportive bandmates and Georgia – and presenter Myleene Klass, Matt's erstwhile jungle campmate.

I'm going to feel naked

It was a strange experience, especially performing without his beloved guitar. He said in anticipation on the show, 'Take your best friends away from you; your instrument away from you, which is like losing a part of your body ... I'm going to feel naked.' He performed impressively though, particularly considering the band were recording *Above the Noise* at the same time. His 'pop voice' and 'opera voice' used different elements of his range, and he had to sing using a completely different method; in the end, he told the boys he couldn't do anything in the studio until the TV show was over – it was too hard to switch between the two. He taught them a few things from his new repertoire, though: cue comedy opera solo from Dougie.

Danny was voted out two weeks from the final, but it was an experience he would never forget.

And *Strictly Come Dancing* looked to be the same for Harry. He certainly had a lot going for him. For a start, he was a professional drummer, so his rhythm was going to be beat-perfect. He had also been a stellar cricketer in his youth at Uppingham, playing for the first team at the age of fourteen and scoring 180 not out; and cricketers had a strong track record on *Strictly*: Darren Gough and Mark Ramprakash had both won previous series thanks to their fancy footwork.

Above all, though, when Harry Judd set his mind to something, he *really* set his mind to it. In *The Making of Radio:ACTIVE* documentary, McFly's producer Jason Perry said of him, 'He's very competitive . . . He wants to be the first and the best at everything.'

It was Alexander Graham Bell who once observed, 'Preparation is the key to success.' And Harry must have known the quote, for he knuckled down to his *Strictly* training with pure focus. He was already at the peak of physical health. As well as having given up alcohol, he'd been training hard for several years to keep himself in shape. He'd run the London Marathon in 2008, raising money for the Teenage Cancer Trust – and his improved physique hadn't gone unnoticed by his bandmates. Tom recalled in *Unsaid Things*,

'I first noticed a difference in him while he was getting changed in his hotel room . . . Cut to ten minutes later, Dougie, Danny and I were all in his room doing press-ups like something out of *The Benny Hill Show*.' That was, indeed, the start of a more active life for all the lads, and they started hiring personal trainers and getting in shape – something Matt Willis was also into in a big way.

Harry also had a secret weapon. Thanks to McFly's close friendship with the Busted boys, he knew James's ex, Kara Tointon, well; and she just happened to have won *Strictly* the year before with an array of show-stopping dances. He spoke to her and got a few insider tips.

He had actually done a one-off *Strictly* special himself, for Children in Need the previous autumn, versus Rochelle Wiseman from the Saturdays. Harry had won, dancing with Ola Jordan (even though he'd tried to persuade the producers to let him dance with Dougie). That experience did give him form, but it also meant that he and his new partner, redhead Aliona Vilani, weren't allowed to start practising until just two weeks before that first cha-cha-cha performance. But come on, this was Harry Judd. Two weeks or not, he nailed it.

And then he was off on the rollercoaster ride that was *Strictly*. Twelve weeks. Fifteen dances. Seventeen stunning performances. All culminating in the Grand Final at the Tower Ballroom in Blackpool, watched by 13 million viewers – and Tom, Danny and Dougie. Danny commented during the show, 'The first time we watched him, we cracked up laughing – and now we're gobsmacked at how good he's dancing.' And Dougie added, 'We're very proud of Harry. It's like when you have a kid and you see your kid playing football for the first time, you're like, "That's my boy."'

And their boy was doing them proud. Harry looked like a matinée idol, sweeping Aliona off her feet into a series of heart-breakingly beautiful lifts throughout the final. Back in 2004, during the '5 Colours in Her Hair' video, an eighteen-year-old Harry had appeared in the black-and-white segment dressed in a smart black suit to present a bouquet of coloured roses; his hair had been slicked back and he looked every inch a debonair heart-throb. That romantic boy was now all grown up. The final saw him perform a quickstep in traditional ballroom tails, and a gorgeous American smooth to 'Can't Help Falling in Love'.

And it seemed the nation couldn't help falling in love with *him* – especially when he and Aliona performed their jive-based show dance to 'Great Balls of Fire', which came complete with a Eurovision, Bucks Fizz-style disrobing from Harry mid-dance, and a drum solo. Judge Bruno Tonioli dubbed him 'dancing royalty', while Len paid homage to the setting by saying, 'If you were a stick of Blackpool rock, you'd have talent written right through you.'

The nerve-racking moment came as host Bruce Forsyth prepared to announce the result. Harry had scored a whopping total of 156 points across his four dances that evening – including two perfect 40s – but the judges' votes didn't count tonight. It was all on the public vote.

Harry and Aliona, still dressed in the costumes from their Argentine tango, stood side by side with actress Chelsee Healey and her partner Pasha Kovalev to hear who had won; like Matt Willis before him, Harry had seen off third-placed Jason Donovan earlier in the night.

And now he saw off Chelsee too. Harry had triumphed. His

bandmates, in typical McFly fashion, stormed the dance floor to congratulate him – scaring the bejesus out of Bruce. Danny leaped into Harry's arms (slightly less gracefully than Aliona had done during the dances) before Tom and Dougie both ran onstage too, and they all enveloped their star drummer in a group hug. Tom later said to the *Daily Record*, 'I think Brucie thought we were streakers. We wanted to streak, but I don't think the BBC would be too happy about that.'

The audience were pleased to see Dougie in particular, because, like Harry, he'd been busy that autumn winning the public's hearts and votes by appearing on *I'm a Celebrity*. The jungle show was the only one he'd ever thought he might do, simply because of the attraction of the Australian wildlife. For lizard-mad Dougie, the idea of spending twenty-one days and nights in the open air with only creepy-crawlies (and fellow celebrities) for company was an appealing one. And so, on 13 November 2011, he'd found himself, just like Matt before him, heading to the jungle for the experience of his life.

Dougie had really admired Matt's whole approach to the show. He said on *I'm a Celebrity Hall of Fame*, 'Matt Willis was probably the best King [of the Jungle] there ever has been. I really felt like he actually enjoyed all the disgusting things he had to eat.' And it wasn't long before Dougie faced those dubious platters himself. Following in Matt's footsteps – and mouthfuls – he ate ostrich anus and bush pig's penis during a Bushtucker Trial,

Matt Willis was probably the best King of the Jungle there ever has been

all washed down with a beverage of emu liver and accompanied by a side order of witchetty grubs. His time in the jungle saw him dress up in a kangaroo costume, be put in the stocks and have water thrown in his face, and – when he was 'king' of the camp – decree that the law of the land was that everyone had to be naked (a popular choice with the viewers back home). He also had to pen a song with his campmates for a round-the-fire singalong with Peter Andre: an easy task for songwriter extraordinaire Dougie. He later named his new 'band' the Leeches, so called 'because we suck'. His old band hadn't forgotten him either: as a reward for one of the tasks, the contestants were allowed a treat and, tongues placed firmly in their cheeks, McFly sent him a picture of Harry in his dancing costume as his 'reward'.

Dougie's campmate Mark Wright, with whom he reached the final, said of him, 'I don't think there was one particular moment when people fell in love with Dougie. I just think you fall in love with Dougie as soon as you see him.' The two of them shared a last, epic, candlelit meal the night before the result was announced – having won an array of tasty dishes thanks to their final Bushtucker Trial – after three weeks of surviving on limited rations. Dougie declared the spread 'sprinkled with magic' and later revealed, 'That was probably the most romantic meal I've ever, ever had.'

On 3 December 2011, Ant and Dec announced the result. Dougie had done it. He was the winner with over 55 per cent of the vote. Mark Wright immediately pulled him into a bear hug and sincerely said, 'There couldn't be a better winner than this man here. He deserves it so much. He's the nicest, kindest person in the whole entire world.'

And while Dougie was 'lost for words', and clearly stunned, others said they'd predicted it from the start. TV presenter Caroline Flack commented in *I'm a Celebrity Hall of Fame*, 'I knew Dougie was going to win even before he went into the jungle. He's got the Matt Willis effect.'

So, like Matt before him, Dougie crossed the famous bridge with his wooden sceptre and his twig coronet, the duly crowned King of the Jungle. He had someone special waiting there for him too. Tom raced through the photographers to sweep him up into a hug. They jumped up and down on the wobbling rope bridge and laughed their heads off. Just months after Dougie's darkest days, he was on top of the world. Tom couldn't have been prouder – and it showed.

It was an achievement that deserved to be marked in a special way. And Danny had just the idea. He posed naked on Twitter with only a small white cup protecting his modesty. When, just a few weeks later, Harry made it a double win for the McFly boys,

> **He posed naked on Twitter with only a small white cup protecting his modesty**

Dougie and Tom joined him in his unique celebrations. The three of them stripped off: Dougie with his tongue out and a platinum disc of *Room on the 3rd Floor* covering himself; Danny with a rock-star wide-mouth gurn and a tiny Union Jack cushion; and Tom looking rather more sheepish, with a larger green cushion in front of his bits. Tom later tweeted, 'I was forced to do this … thanks for voting!' But the others showed no such regrets. Danny tweeted, 'We said we would do it!' and Dougie posted a typically amusing message: 'As promised . . . you pervs!'

They took to Twitter to champion the double win, too. Dougie, so recently crowned King of the Jungle, said, 'I have a queen! Thanks so much guys! This is ace!' And Harry told BBC Radio 5 Live that what they'd done was 'a McDouble'. He added, 'What an amazing year, we never ever expected it. We are two happy lads.'

There were two happy lads in the Willis household, too. As Dougie was getting to grips with the Australian tucker and Harry was tackling his tango, Matt and Emma announced the arrival of their second child on 25 November: a son, whom they named Ace Billy Willis. Matt said of the middle name on Twitter, 'Went for Billy so if he wants to be like a f**king banker or something he can use that instead!'

Matt definitely wasn't a banker. He was still dazzling the musical-theatre world with his impressive rock voice – and his acting, which was improving with every role he took. Now, after a series of eight or nine intense auditions, he landed the part of Fiyero in one of the West End's most successful shows, *Wicked*. Not for the first time in his life, Matt was playing the love interest.

And he had a partner in crime in musical-theatre land too. James, having first tested the water with that early commission for the Youth Music Theatre, was fast becoming a force to be reckoned with. He'd written another musical with Elliot Davis, *Out There*, and also learned that their original show, *Loserville*, would have a full professional run at the West Yorkshire Playhouse in the summer of 2012 – starring none other than Gareth Gates, who had used to perform at the same Party in the Park gigs as Busted back in the day.

For Tom, there was only one 'gig' that summer that mattered. On Saturday, 12 May, he made his way to One Marylebone, a Grade I-listed former church near Regent's Park in London, to marry the girl of his dreams. The night before, his stag do had featured his old Busted audition video coming out of the closet as McFly had a good laugh about old times. And now his bandmates – his best mates – played the role of his best men.

They all wore tailored suits with fresh green ties. Giovanna, meanwhile, looked stunning. The Italian good looks that had caught Tom's eye in assembly all those years ago had blossomed. She was a simply beautiful bride. Gi wore her dark hair down, tumbling around her shoulders in gentle waves. Her strapless gown was by Phillipa Lepley, with a beaded belt and an overlay of the most exquisite vintage lace. She carried a bouquet of blowsy pink blooms, with classic cascading ivy. Harry's Izzy played 'Somewhere Over the Rainbow' on her violin as Gi walked down the aisle to meet her groom.

Afterwards, but before McFly played as the wedding band, there was the small matter of Tom's speech. He wasn't good at public speaking. The thought of giving a speech in front of all the wedding guests, who included Matt and Emma, and Kara Tointon, who was a bridesmaid, was too nerve-racking for words. He preferred to sing.

So he'd asked Danny, in top secret, to arrange some backing music for him: a medley of McFly's greatest hits. He stood up, introduced himself and what he was about to do, and then performed what can only be described as one of the greatest groom wedding-day speeches of all time. For fourteen minutes, he held his audience captivated as he acknowledged the help of his family and friends in musical form. He almost broke down as he thanked Dougie, Danny and Harry to the tune of 'Room on the 3rd Floor' – the song that he'd written so long ago with Danny at the InterContinental. But, in the end, it was all about Gi, set to the music of 'All About You'. Current students from Sylvia Young filed into the room behind him to sing as a choir as the song reached its

> **He performed what can only be described as one of the greatest groom wedding-day speeches of all time**

climax. There wasn't a dry eye in the house. Tom later said to the *Mirror*, 'Danny was really crying. I've never seen that; he doesn't cry a lot. So he set me off.'

And it was perhaps Danny who summed it up best of all in the best-man speech, which he delivered with Harry and Dougie. Quoted in *OK!*, he said, 'We'd like to finish off by saying that you two bring out the best in each other . . . You really are the best of mates and that's why we know that this true love story will last forever.'

As Gi and Tom jetted off to St Lucia for their honeymoon, the true love story of the McFly boys began another chapter. Travelling with the newlyweds were Harry and Izzy. As they landed at the airport on the tropical island, Harry and Tom had a secret rendezvous in the airport loos – so Tom could give Harry back the engagement ring he'd carried for him, just in case customs had asked Harry to open his luggage and had spoiled the surprise.

'When we got [to our accommodation], I thought he was

acting strangely,' Izzy later remembered to *Hello!*. 'We were getting ready and I was like, "Come on, let's get dinner, I'm hungry." He said, "No, not yet," and started dancing around the room with me.' He then led Izzy along a candlelit path to the beach, where a table was set for them. 'We hadn't even had [time for] a drink and Harry was down on one knee,' Izzy said with a smile, while Harry recalled, 'I was suddenly nervous. I was shaking a bit and when I opened the box the ring was upside down.'

Somehow that was apt – for this woman had turned his world upside down. They married just seven months later, on Friday, 21 December 2012, in Izzy's home town of Harpenden in Hertfordshire. The McFly boys were ushers, wearing silver waistcoats and pale pink ties to match the bridesmaids' gowns; Matt, Emma and Kara were all guests once again.

It was a magical winter wedding. Harry looked as dapper as on his *Strictly* days in black tails with an ivory silk waistcoat and tie. And Izzy was his picture-perfect partner in a bespoke full-length dress fashioned from Chantilly lace, silk georgette and taffeta, made by Tantrums & Tiaras in Putney, London. She had her chestnut hair pinned half up and half down, with a sparkling headpiece nestling beneath her snow-white veil. She and Harry held hands throughout the ceremony – one so moving it prompted both Tom and Danny to cry. It included a special performance from Dougie, Tom and Danny on acoustic guitars, as they performed the Beach Boys' classic 'Don't Worry Baby' for the newlyweds. McFly performed four songs at the wedding reception, too.

The night, though, belonged to Izzy and Harry. As Alan Dedicoat's voice introduced them, they performed an unforgettable

American smooth – complete with lifts – as their first dance, and waltzed into a wonderful future.

The year ahead, 2013, looked bright. And it started with new music. In February, James Bourne joined McFly for a writing trip in Wales. His musical *Loserville* had transferred to the West End in the winter – Danny, Dougie, Harry and Matt's wife Emma had all attended the premiere – and he was spending a bit more time in the UK of late, performing a solo acoustic tour, overseeing the West End transfer, and writing with Tom, Danny, Dougie and Harry. They all uploaded a new song, 'My TVR', to YouTube in the spring. Tom and Danny strummed their acoustic guitars as McFly debuted the summery track, which was full of the soaring harmonies and catchy vocals people had come to expect from the band. Their musical experiment was over. They were back at their best.

James was embracing Twitter, too. Some time ago, he'd tweeted, 'My DeLorean will fly one day! Mark my words.' This from a man who'd once said in *Busted on Tour*, 'When I promise myself something, it happens.'

James's promise to himself was about to come true – and far, far sooner than he might have thought.

THIRTEEN

Don't Let It Go to Waste

The Manchester Apollo, a Grade II-listed, Art Deco theatre, first opened as a cinema in August 1938. It was the sort of film fact that might have appealed to James Bourne, but he was too stoked about seeing his good friends McFly to worry too much about the provenance of the building they were in. He hurried backstage.

It had been a busy few days. He'd jetted over from New York, where he was still living – currently hard at work on a brand-new musical, *Murder at the Gates*, which he was writing with the Tony Award winner Steven Sater – in order to attend the Olivier Awards, the West End's most prestigious awards ceremony. *Loserville*, against all odds, had been nominated as Best New Musical.

It was an accolade that blew James's mind. Simply having a

show on in the West End was mad enough in itself. As James said to The Vault, 'Three years ago [the show] was nothing, just an idea. To get here [to the West End] is crazier than anything. The chances are so slim.' To make it happen, he'd had to channel everything into it. He later revealed to heatworld.com, 'I could have written songs for One Direction' – which was something Tom, Dougie and Danny were doing – 'or I could have done *Loserville*.' And for James, there was no contest. He said to The Vault, '[Writing for other people is] not as fulfilling as being on the inside of a project, as I was [when I was writing] with McFly – we shared a vision – or with my own band.' He summed it up to heatworld.com, '[With *Loserville*] I get to be more creative.'

I could have written songs for One Direction

And that investment in his own creativity had now paid off. He'd been invited to perform at the Olivier Awards, so the previous evening he'd been singing 'Holly . . . I'm the One' to the crème de la crème of British the-atre, dressed in an unusually debonair outfit, for James, of a black tie, smart white shirt, grey waistcoat and trousers. Despite the elegant look, he delivered a performance that bore all the hall-marks of his usual high-energy routines. He even rocked out an old-school Busted jump with his legs splayed dramatically. His former Son of Dork bandmate, Danny Hall, had joined him on drums. They were the only two left from the original SOD line-up now.

James had started a new band recently. He and his brother Chris – who had also become a musician: a bassist in the band

Hollywood Ending – had teamed up to form the Bourne Insanity. So far, though, they'd released only one track: 'Mohawk'.

So James was also doing his own thing: playing a small solo acoustic tour and, as ever, writing new music. He reflected on the stark difference of performing his music these days to The Vault. 'You don't appreciate at the time [of Busted] how incredible it is that that many people are coming to see your band every night [in arenas]. It's such a surreal thing.

'Now if I play a gig I'm lucky if I pack out the Islington Academy.'

Still, he was slowly finding some peace about the Busted split. He and Matt had even built some bridges with Charlie. James told The Vault, 'We went round to Charlie's house [in September 2012] . . . It was strange . . . The three of us had not hung out since we split up. It was the first time.'

Some things hadn't changed, though. James continued, 'He said to us there and then [that] there was no sign of him showing any interest [in a reunion] . . . no sign that he was remotely interested.'

But the Busted reunion rumours kept on coming. Even Louis Tomlinson from One Direction had joined in, tweeting plaintively: 'I have to say back in the day Busted f**king smashed it. Come on @mattjwillis @charliesimo @jamesbourne just do one more gig!'

Matt, for one, was certainly conscious of the clock ticking as his and James's thirtieth birthdays approached. He said to The Vault, 'Singing "What I Go to School For" when I'm thirty-five is not cool. Maybe we need to do it sooner rather than later. Or maybe I just dismiss it as some crazy thought at the back of my head and it belongs there.' Going solo wasn't something he wanted to do again either: 'I found being onstage [as a solo artist] quite . . . not hard . . . but definitely I felt I was more comfortable as a member of a group rather than as a solo artist.'

Shit-hot TV producers, their fingers firmly on the pop-culture pulse, clocked the uprising of interest in Busted coming back – but Matt and James weren't keen on the kind of opportunities being suggested to them. James tweeted frankly, 'Busted and [the TV reality-documentary show] *The Big Reunion* is like custard and mashed potatoes in the same bowl. A really bad idea.' He went into more detail on The Vault, saying, 'There's a difference behind the way we think about stuff. Even though we were a boy band, and people put us in the boy-band [category] . . . and we were marketed no different from a boy band, the thought behind how we do our music is not the same.'

And, frustratingly, music was something he and Matt really, really wanted to do together. It had been almost three years since they'd recorded those six tracks that Matt had mentioned on *This Morning* – and not one of them had ever seen the light of day.

At Matt's house one day that spring, Matt had turned to James and said, 'Listen. This is stupid. I want to do music with you.'

The feeling was mutual.

It should have been so simple.

But the solution to their problems was not.

Yet it wasn't something that James was going to worry about today. He was here in Manchester to hang with McFly, who were eight gigs into their *Memory Lane* tour, promoting the second greatest-hits album of their career. With 2013 being the band's ten-year anniversary since they'd first formed, they'd finally reached the magic number that Tom had felt was suitable, in that interview all those years ago, to release a compilation of their hits. *Memory Lane* had come out at the end of last year. Now, they were touring the album.

James bumped fists with them as he joined them backstage. There was Dougie, chilled and looking cool as ever. He'd started two skater-style clothing ranges now, Zukie and Saint Kidd, just as James had done before him with Sic Puppy in his Busted days. Danny and Harry were there, too, getting ready for the gig. And there was Tom, perhaps faffing about with a video camera, preparing one of his vlogs. There was more reason than ever now to make them good, because Tom had unexpectedly become a viral Internet sensation. He had uploaded the video of his unique wedding speech to YouTube at the start of the year, and it had attracted millions upon millions upon millions of hits – almost 14 million and counting.

In a way, it wasn't surprising: anyone who watched the video couldn't help but connect with it emotionally. There is something about music that hits you right in the solar plexus, anyway; and the soul-stirring melodies he'd chosen, plus the heart-rending nature of a wedding speech in itself, combined to provoke a stratospherically emotional effect. Tom, close to tears as he thanked

> **Tom had unexpectedly become a viral Internet sensation**

his parents and his best friends, seemed to encapsulate everything we all experience in life but often fail to find the words to express.

Somehow, he was doing it for us. And so, as the frog in his throat leaped higher with his tribute to Danny, Harry and Dougie, each of the viewers watching thought of their best friends, and teared up too. It was such an accomplished, yet simultaneously genuine, speech. Tom's love for Giovanna was as crystal clear as the champagne flutes with which their wedding guests toasted them; and a bit like 'All About You' itself – a bespoke track for Gi that had connected with thousands of people and in turn become *their* special song – Tom's wedding speech had the gift of universality by being utterly personal.

The first James knew of his friend's spectacularly risen profile was when he'd been on a writing trip with the gang. He remembered backstage at the Jingle Bell Ball in Belfast, 'I knew it was quite serious when we were in Wales writing songs and Tom was disappearing to talk to the news [in America] about his wedding tape. We were like, "When are we going to finish this song? Where's Tom?" And we're like, "Oh, he's on the news talking about his YouTube video."'

Even Oscar-winning actor Russell Crowe had seen it, and experienced that connection that every viewer seemed to have. He commented to Magic FM, 'I sat and watched that [video] and what came to my mind was, "I've just met one of the richest men in the world. That man has such a rich internal life . . ." I think he's incredibly special and I'll be very interested in whatever else he's going to do.'

What he was doing at the moment was getting ready to rock the Manchester Apollo. The band were psyched about this tour. They were playing all their greatest hits, and it was the perfect full stop before they started recording their sixth album. They were planning to head to Texas – with producer Jason Perry back onboard – to record it after the tour was over.

They'd been writing new songs for the album for a while now, and James was over from the States in part to see if any on-tour magic might happen, just like in the old days. Manchester had been the scene of some top writing in the past – 'Air Hostess', 'Who's David?' and 'Unsaid Things' had all been written in the city – so it seemed only right that it was at this particular venue that he'd happened to hook up with them.

Also hanging backstage that night were an up-and-coming band called the Vamps, who would be releasing their debut single in the coming September. James, Tom, Dougie and Danny would all write with the band for their debut album, but its release was many months away yet. This day, Friday, 3 May 2013, the Vamps were here to warm up the crowd for McFly as their support act – just as McFly had done for Busted many moons ago.

The Manchester Apollo holds 3,500 people. James, Tom, Danny, Dougie and Harry could hear them all coming into the old cinema on that Friday night, raucously up for a good time and energised about the evening's entertainment. With Bolton's Danny Jones in the band, playing Manchester was like playing a home crowd: the atmosphere would be electric.

The fans' chatter and excitement vibrated through the Art Deco walls, through to where the band were kicking back in their dressing room. As usual, they were having a laugh. This was the band who had donned fake moustaches to play a cheesy restaurant trio in the 'Sorry's Not Good Enough' video; who had recorded a bespoke 'Star Boy' track for Chris Moyles on his departure from Radio 1, complete with comedy scene of them in bed together; whose latest video, for 'Love Is Easy', had given a starring role to a pink ukulele and restaged their respective reality-show wins in am-dram fashion. Having a laugh was in their DNA.

'Hey, James.'

An idea was brewing.

'What?'

'Mate, wouldn't it be funny if you went out there and played a few songs?'

It had been a long time since he'd heard screams like these. James slowly walked out onto the stage, a lonely silhouette against the backlight. He stood before a microphone in front of the Vamps' drum kit. They hadn't performed yet. It was just him. He had his black guitar strap across his shoulder, and his acoustic guitar in his arms.

It had been a long time since he'd heard screams like these

He stood still for a second, thinking, letting the moment wash over him, and then he started strumming his guitar. There was only one light on the stage, picking out the drum kit and the black curtains behind him that concealed McFly's set. He played into the darkness.

As it always did, the music shot into his veins. He found himself swaying gently in time as the song built. He was James from Busted, but he was also James the singer-songwriter from New York, James from Southend-on-Sea, James who wrote songs in his bedroom, and wanted people to hear them any way they could.

His vocal started. And the lights came up. He was dressed in a simple T-shirt and khaki trousers, with a blue checked shirt over the top. He wasn't in full leathers or boy-band garb, but the screams that greeted him suggested otherwise. He sang on. 'Beautiful Girls Are the Loneliest' was a relatively new track. But this was an artist who had played arenas when he was just twenty years old. He'd sold out Wembley eleven times. And he had a list of songwriting credits for top-ten hits as long as his arm. By the end of the song, every one of those 3,500 people was singing along. He played the crowd just as well as he played guitar. They were chorusing his music back at him, just as they used to do. Though he kept it together for the song, James couldn't resist the smile that tugged playfully at his lips. This felt good.

Tom, Dougie, Danny and Harry were watching him from the side of the stage. Tom remembered on *McBusted: The Birth*, 'It was really exciting for us because it was the first time we'd really seen James and seen him play anything for a while.' Harry remembered that they were 'really apprehensive to see what it was like'.

What it was like was, well, something else. Having got the crowd on side with a new song, James took a step back in time. He took things more uptempo by quickly segueing into 'Everything I Knew', a song he and Matt had written together for Busted's first album. To the rapid rhythm of his own accompaniment, he ran through the track. The crowd's support was visceral. At the end of the first chorus, James couldn't help himself. When his enthusiastic 'Woo!' was met with 3,500 screams, he jumped up and down onstage with sheer excitement. The shiny whites of his teeth, glistening through his wide smile, could have been seen from the balcony. As the song came to an end, he shouted, 'Yeah!' exultantly and the audience screamed their heads off.

People say cheesily, 'Feel the love in the room.' James could have reached out and touched it in the Apollo that night. He paused for a moment. 'I want to thank McFly,' he said, which set the screaming off again, 'for having me up here. We've been writing songs together again. And they're coming out quite good.'

There was time for just one more good song of his own. He started playing a little guitar lick. It was familiar and yet not; a bit more staccato, a few more flourishes, much less production. James was completely straight-faced. What was it? Another new track?

Tom, still standing by the side of the stage, happily taking in the scene of his friend just storming it, remembered on *McBusted: The Birth*, 'He started playing this riff, and we were like, "What song is this?" It kind of sounded a bit like "Year 3000" . . . Could have been, was it . . .? There were murmurings around the audience. And then he started singing "Year 3000" and it. Just. Went. Nuts.'

The audience's shrieks hit ear-splitting levels. And as soon as they'd run out of air from that first breathless scream, they started singing with him. He was only fifteen words in and he didn't need to keep going – the crowd were crooning it for him, word-perfect ten years on from the song's debut. James let their energy carry him from one side of the stage to the other, as he bounded in huge gallops across the stage, no longer needing to stay near the mic when the audience were the ones making enough noise to lift the rafters.

Looking out into the crowd, he could see a sea of smartphones recording shaky home movies of his moment of glory. Everyone could sense this was musical history in the making, and they wanted a record to keep for ever. When the chorus hit, those who weren't already dancing leaped to their feet and sang even louder.

James was in his element. He'd feed in the odd line but the crowd didn't need it. He swung his head in time with the music and kicked the air as the climax rounded the corner. He was up there on his own, without a band – but the 3,500 people stepped into the breach. As they kept the

Everyone could sense this was music history in the making

chorus going, James freestyled over the top of them. It was a masterclass. This wasn't some has-been, riding a wave of nostalgia: this was a musical maestro at the top of his game, finally getting recognition for writing songs that had lasted much, much longer than anyone had given him credit for back in the day. James recalled on *McBusted: The Birth*, 'It didn't feel like I was playing for someone else's fans. It felt like the McFly fans were also Busted fans. It felt like a home crowd. It felt like a Busted audience.'

Tom added, 'It was like Busted had never been gone.'

As the song reached its final stages, people started screaming again. They took it to another level when James freestyled the words 'crashed the wedding' – but he was teasing them. Like any good showman, he left them wanting more. With a simple, shouted 'Thank you!' he unplugged his guitar and walked off the stage. The lights faded to black.

It was perhaps Dougie who summed it up best. He said on *McBusted: The Birth*: 'I'm not ashamed to say it, but it was magical.'

*

Reflecting in his room at the hotel that night, James couldn't believe it. The reaction had been so incredible.

There was only one small fly in the ointment. Years ago, he'd commented to the *Birmingham Mail*, 'Being in a band is more fun [than being solo]. When you win stuff and do well, it's better to say "We did it" rather than "I did it". It's better to share the experience. If you're solo, you're alone. If you've done something good, you've got no one to have a beer or relate the experience with afterwards.'

There was a knock on his door. It was Fletch. James remembered on *The Jonathan Ross Show*, 'Our manager came up to the hotel room. He showed me a long list of arena dates.'

James was flummoxed. He stared at Fletch, who'd always given him such good advice; who'd been the one to persuade him to stay with Rashman, back when Busted were first starting out; who'd had the commercial and creative vision to build not only Busted but also McFly into a world-class band. Fletch just watched him look through the dates.

Arenas? He'd barely sold out the 800-seater Islington Academy last time he'd gone on tour. He shook his head in disbelief.

Fletch spoke at last. 'The promoters believe you can do this.'

And he wouldn't be alone.

FOURTEEN

Ticket Outta Loserville

'Let's go!'

Danny yelled into the mic, as Tom launched into the classic guitar riff that opened 'Saturday Night'. Almost ten years ago, it had been the first track they'd ever played in front of an audience, when they'd supported Busted on their arena tour. Tonight, it was the first track to open their ten-year-anniversary celebrations, as McFly played four nights at the prestigious Royal Albert Hall in September 2013.

And there was a lot to celebrate. One of the band in particular had had some special news of late. In July, Danny had asked Georgia to marry him while they were on a sun-kissed holiday in Cyprus. He'd arranged a romantic beach setting, with a five-course meal prepared especially for them – and a glittering De Beers engagement ring hidden under the table. Georgia told

Hello! that he'd started the proposal by asking her when she wanted to get married. She'd joked in reply, 'Well, when you bloomin' propose.'

'What about if I do it now?' returned Danny.

Georgia confessed, 'With that I put my head in my hands and started bawling. When I looked up, he was down on one knee in front of me, tears billowing out of his eyes, and he said, "Will you be my future Mrs Jones?"'

The wedding was set for the following summer in Georgia's native Yorkshire – as Danny put it to the *Bolton News*, 'The wrong side of the Pennines . . . sorry about that.' He'd already asked his bandmates to be his best men. He said to *Hello!*, 'We're like brothers. Our backgrounds are so different but we all get on so amazingly well. We have a connection on another level to everything else.'

Will you be my future Mrs Jones?

And they were certainly connecting onstage tonight. Their die-hard fans were treated to an explosive array of all their hit songs. Chris Moyles appeared in a VT to introduce 'Star Girl', explaining how he'd first met McFly 'when Busted gave birth to you all those years ago'. The band finally indulged seven years' worth of requests when they played 'Little Joanna', a soaring ice-cream sundae of a song from *Motion in the Ocean*, which was as musically complex as it was toe-tappingly terrific, and which they'd never had the balls to play live before in case they, well, ballsed it up. It was simply glorious, and the crowd joined in with the rhythmic backing vocals as the lights shimmered. And Dougie – it would be Dougie, of course – got to play the Albert Hall's world-famous organ for the dramatic introduction to 'Transylvania'.

It was indeed the perfect venue to mark the occasion, packed full of history as well as heaving bodies. As the strains of 'Love Is Easy' – played on Tom's pink ukulele – faded out, the lights dimmed, too. And so the scene was set, ready and waiting, for a new chapter of music history to be made.

An idea had been born back in May at the Manchester Apollo. Harry summarised it backstage at the Jingle Bell Ball: 'James came on tour with us to write some songs and hang out, and we said, "Why don't you go onstage and sing some Busted songs acoustically? It'll be a laugh, we'll watch and have a giggle." And he did it and the reaction was insane and we were like, "This is awesome, how can we make this a reality?"' He expanded to The Vault, 'It was so fun to watch and the crowd reaction was so special that we were like, "Why don't we just be the band, why don't we just be one band?"'

James took up the story. 'The theory was, if I can go onstage at a McFly show and play Busted songs and have it go down as well as it went down, surely if Matt came on [too] it would be even better . . . and surely if we all just slayed, it would be *even* better than that . . . It was an idea that happened between all of us . . . After [I played we were like], "Oh my God, there has to be a way."'

As the saying goes, where there's a will, there's a way. James said to The Vault that, before Manchester, he and Matt had been 'willing something to happen' to help them reunite. The perfect opportunity had just landed in their laps.

The McFly anniversary was a focal point and an excuse to do

something really special, and the reaction of the crowd at the Apollo was too extraordinary to ignore. Danny said on *McBusted: The Birth*, 'We wanted to have guests [at the Royal Albert Hall] and the first people that came to mind were Matt and James and we asked them ... and they said yes.' The timing of James's impromptu gig couldn't have been better. And so, that summer, it wasn't just McFly who rehearsed for the high-profile gigs. They had a couple of friends along for the ride too.

The audience in the Albert Hall that night first got an inkling of what was to come when the screens flickered to life and a VT rolled, just over fifty minutes into the gig. There were Matt and James onscreen, talking about McFly. Huge cheers went up for the Busted boys – just as they had for James at the Apollo. Matt mused to the camera, 'I remember meeting Danny for the first time and knowing that those two [he and Tom] had a real connection,' while James reminisced, 'It was amazing to have both bands on the road together [for the arena tour]. That was a really good time.'

As the screens faded to black, it was black too inside the Albert Hall. The girls' screams punctured the dark. Almost ten seconds passed. Silence from the stage. Then, through the darkness, the unmistakeable bass line of 'Year 3000' kicked in. The lights throbbed once, like a new dawn, and then resumed their shadowy swirls, obscuring exactly who was onstage.

As the lead guitar ripped into the main riff, pixelated lights at the back of the stage spelled out one word, very briefly, against the back wall, before it was blasted away by a shower of sparkling pyrotechnics.

McBusted.

As the lights came up fully, there were six very talented, very excited, very animated musicians onstage – and they were determined to have F.U.N. Already they were bouncing dementedly up and down onstage as if they were at a pogo-stick convention (all except Harry, who was having the time of his life bashing his drum kit to Busted's rocky music). In a sign of things to come, Danny, James and Matt split the six-line first verse into three parts, with each of them taking lead vocals; there were no divas in this band, and Danny took the first line to showcase that this really was a supergroup and not just Busted on their own, back for one last gig.

> **Pixelated lights at the back of the stage spelled out one word: McBusted**

As the bridge to the chorus came in, James and Tom, old friends that they were, did the honours, harmonising on adjacent mics, while Matt went insane, leaping and spinning and doing Busted jumps next to Dougie in a seemingly school-uniform-inspired outfit: school striped tie, short-sleeved white shirt and a sleeveless denim jacket with patches. James was in shorts and his trusty checked shirt, this time in red and black, mirroring Tom who was in a bluey-grey checked shirt. Danny was in rock-star black, Dougie in purple-bandana heaven and a patterned shirt, and Harry in a grey New Order T-shirt. A marketing exec would have thrown his hands up in horror at the lack of coordination – but it absolutely worked. These were six friends up there having a blast, being true to themselves, and showing harmony in more than just the music.

As the chorus of 'Year 3000' kicked in, all five guitarists were on their mics, singing away as the crowd went wild, with Tom throwing in some new harmonies. The atmosphere in the Albert Hall was extraordinary. Harry later said emphatically on *McBusted: The Birth*, 'I've tried to take nothing for granted over the past ten years. One thing I definitely don't take for granted is the crowds that we play to. They're always incredible, the fans are insane, they're so loud; there's always an amazing atmosphere at our [McFly] gigs.

'But when we went out for the Royal Albert Hall shows for our ten-year anniversary, when Matt and James came out and "Year 3000" started, I think it's arguably the biggest screams and feeling of electricity in a venue that I've *ever* felt before. It was such a special moment.'

And magic moments were happening onstage at a rate of knots. When you have five vocalists on a Busted song rather than just three, the musical arrangements know no bounds. Dougie chipped in every now and again on his favourite bits – especially when James raced over to his mic and they tag-teamed lines.

> **It was the biggest feeling of electricity in a venue that I've *ever* felt before**

McFly were clearly enjoying rocking out to the Busted song. Having five singers also meant there was more chance for Danny to get into his guitar riffs as he played along with James's vocals, or for Tom to jump crazily up and down while someone else sang. Matt Willis was just beaming as the crowd chanted the chorus at him ('Say what?' he yelled at them), and you could hear the laughter in his voice as he sang, bubbling up from inside of him and helplessly out into the lyrics.

The McBusted name was up in lights at the back of the Albert Hall as the band performed in front of it, each letter picked out in golden pixelated dots. And the audience went absolutely dotty as the iconic aeroplane roar that signalled the start of 'Air Hostess' zoomed around the Albert Hall's speakers. The lighting design switched to bright backlighting as the two bassists – Matt and Dougie – faced each other down to duet on the iconic bass line. James and Danny shared the spoken intro, and then James took lead vocals for the first verse. His foot beat in time as he held his arm aloft, while Tom, crouched next to him, had his head bowed and low, concentrating intently on his guitar licks.

James and Matt found each other when Tom took over the vocals and rocked out face to face on their guitars. Matt would later say on *McBusted: The Birth*, 'It was awesome, it felt right, it felt good – and it just felt great seeing James on a microphone [just] over there [from me]. And it felt right being on a stage with McFly as well. It felt homely.'

'Homely' wasn't quite the adjective the audience would have used. The unholy union of McFly and Busted was proving to be shockingly explosive, high-energy and super, super fun. Danny and Dougie couldn't help singing along even when they weren't on vocals. The five of them out front ran, jumped, strode and spun across the stage. Even Dougie took a whole section to sing on his own. It was irrepressibly entertaining. Tom was head-banging as he played his guitar. This was the first time he'd ever played the song he'd co-written in front of an audience; he and McFly had used it for sound checks in the past, but that definitely didn't count. What counted was this unique, special rendition of a near-ten-year-old song, which had aged as well as the whisky Dougie used to neck night after night.

The audience screamed harder as the five of them onstage, on cue, did a massive, collective jump into the final chorus. Danny freestyled over the top as the others sang along, layering the sound like groupies in a bed. The band simply looked like five very, very cool guys with guitars. And, while the music was at times shouted rather than sung, everyone was having far too much fun to care. Wouldn't anyone scream their head off if they were let loose on the stage to sing 'Air Hostess' in front of 5,000 fans?

As the guitarists gathered round Harry's drums for the climax to the track, James wheeled his arms like Elvis. There were new Kings of Rock and Roll now – and they were called McBusted.

Harry stretched his arms high and brought them crashing down on his cymbals to finish the song. The lights went to black-out. There was a full-throated laugh from someone on the stage in the darkness – maybe Matt. Maybe any of them. They were all beaming from their faces to their toes, and their expressions mir-rored those of their audience, many of whom had raised their fingers to the air to fashion a heart shape in silhouette. The guys' pleasure in their performance, and in performing with each other, was tangible – especially when James, Matt and Tom briefly took to the mics to greet each other (cue crazy screams). Matt was the one who got the rock-star moment: 'Hello, Royal Albert Hall!'

And with that it was time for another song. 'Shine a Light' is anthemic at the best of times. Tonight, it heralded the start of something new, and shone a light into the future. James and

Danny faced each other to play their guitars as Tom took the first vocals. Matt was at the front of the stage, rocking out with the crowd. Danny and James took over the vocals for the bridge, James harmonising with Danny's voice. And it was Matt who landed the soaring chorus. His musical-theatre training lifted his vocals higher than a bird's, and he sang with his eyes squeezed shut, relishing the moment. The lyric might have been about being on his own, but he was anything but. He had a whole band alongside him.

For James and Tom, the song was an opportunity to jam together. Shoulder to shoulder, comrades and guitars in arms, they played their hearts out. Matt knelt before Dougie as they played their basses with obvious enthusiasm. As Matt took the chorus again, McFly were bouncing off the walls and on the stage – up and down, up and down. James joined his old band-mate on the 'yeah' moments, and then Danny lifted his mic stand high in the air to capture the chorusing of the crowd.

As the song segued into a slower segment, the lights turned blue and Tom took things down a notch as his softer voice carried the song. James, getting lost in the moment, let the occasion run away with him and started moonwalking in a circle, just like his idol Michael Jackson. Harry, looking over his drums towards the singers, caught him at it and smiled knowingly to himself at his bandmate's batty behaviour.

And then the beat kicked in strongly again, Harry beat the life out of the drums and the five guitarists – on Danny's command of 'Jump, jump!' – went back to the unified bouncing. The call-and-return split of the chorus was divided up between them, James and Tom on one part while the others did the rest. Matt and Danny had a rock-voice-off at the end, splitting the final lines of the song between them as James and Tom jammed on their guitars. But they were both winners. Fun and energy zoomed off the stage, rattled round every one of the 9,997 speaking pipes of the Albert Hall's organ and hit the famous flying saucers of the roof. It was somehow apt for such a sci-fi-mad band.

Fun and energy zoomed off the stage

They were nearing the end now. They gathered round Harry's drums again. From left to right: Tom, James, Danny, Matt, Dougie. On cue, they leaped into the air – McBusted united – and landed as one. McBusted had arrived.

The lights faded to black. For almost a full minute, the stage was dark and no music played. All the audience could hear was some indistinct excited chatter. It didn't take much to imagine the high-fives being exchanged by the six members of the new band.

The set had lasted a little over twelve minutes in total.

McBusted would last a little longer than that.

Monday, 11 November 2013, wasn't a particularly chilly day – it was a mild 7 degrees Celsius on the bustling London streets outside – but the atmosphere inside the stunned press-conference room at the Soho Hotel was as warm as hot fudge sauce, and just as sweet.

One by one, McBusted filed into the room. Danny led the way, followed by Dougie, Matt, James, Tom and Harry; the McFly boys sandwiching two-thirds of Busted between them. On the wall behind the band, an image was projected. It had the height chart from Busted's iconic debut album artwork – except this time, instead of showcasing three criminally good musicians, there were six. Stamped across it, in bright red, was the new McBusted logo.

The guys needed someone to introduce them and run the Q&A. Someone like an experienced TV presenter who had just landed the main *Big Brother* presenting job would be good. Happily, Matt Willis was married to her. Emma welcomed the journalists and cracked a couple of jokes about it being 'bring your wife to work' day.

And then the guys revealed the news to end all news: McBusted were going on a rip-roaring, all-rocking, sextet-tastic tour. Eleven dates. Eleven arenas. Six bandmates.

It was going to be carnage.

For James, it was the most exciting news ever. So exciting, in fact, that he'd been camped out at the Soho Hotel for the past two days, just counting down to this very press conference. He said to the assembled journalists, 'I was like a really excited kid [ready] to go on holiday, with my backpack [on, waiting] in the car . . . the flight wasn't till Monday, but I checked in on Friday.'

And now they were all ready to rock and roll.

James announced the news on his Facebook page: 'I'm back in a band, and not just any band, a superband. McBusted will be touring from April next year. Get your tickets from Friday 15 November 2013.'

It was going to be carnage

The pop world was agog at the news. The biggest talking point was the name. McBusted? *Really?* As the Backstreet Boys would later famously say, 'It sounds like a sandwich.' Were they a band or a burger?

It was something the guys themselves were all too aware of. Matt Willis, for one, hadn't even anticipated that the new band would have a name. He said to *Showbiz 411*, 'I never thought it was going to be called McBusted. I thought it was going to be "Busted and McFly play the hits of Busted and McFly."'

Harry interrupted the interview to make a correction: 'McFly and Busted.'

Perhaps it was just as well a new name had been created . . .

So McBusted it was – somehow. Matt said to a fan in a YouTube interview, 'It was like, in the meantime, before we think of something cool, we'll just call it McBusted . . . and then [we were like], "Oh, we've announced the tour [and we're all being interviewed] – oh no!"' Too late. He added to *5 NewsTalk Live*, 'I always thought it was a joke, and that someone was going to come up with something better, but it just kind of stuck, and now we are McBusted for ever.' James joked to the same fan as Matt, 'Does it look like we thought hard about our name?'

PopJustice.com had an opinion, saying, 'We'd argue that the trick with these compound names is that neither name should appear in full, which is why McFlusted is about 87 per cent better than McBusted, but it's too late to change so there you go.'

The band were sticking to their guns. Harry explained the reasoning behind it to *Showbiz 411*. They hadn't just plucked it out of the air; a little bit of brainstorming had gone on. He said, 'It's like Busted-Fly, Bust-Fly – it doesn't work. McBusted just works.' Danny added in a fan video, 'There was just no other choice.' As was so often the case, it was Tom who settled the matter once and for all: 'When people would refer to us they'd naturally call us McBusted, and it just kind of stuck.' And there was one member of the new group who had almost known from the start that this was the way it had to be. For Harry, whose friends had used to rib him about McFly being a mini 'McBusted', the name seemed like fate.

People couldn't help but notice the significance of the venue for the announcement: the Soho Hotel was the location where Busted had chosen, in 2005, to reveal they were splitting up. Earlier in 2013 – in January – James had given a solo interview to The Vault, and it was still too painful for him to talk about it, even then. He'd said, 'Yeah, upset doesn't really cut it. I can't even watch the video of the conference because it's just ... it's a lot ...' His voice had petered out.

This was one video he was going to want to watch over and over again. He said to Showbiz 411, 'We loved being in the band and were sad for it to end. But this is such a surprise that we even get to do this again. This is really exciting for us.'

It was now or never

Matt, at the press conference, acknowledged the significance of the venue. 'It's good to be here for something positive, because last time was quite depressing,' he deadpanned.

James, meanwhile, was disbelieving at their good fortune. 'We didn't think we'd ever come back. We never thought that we would ever play any of this music ever again.'

As Matt put it on McBusted: The Birth, 'It was now or never.' The clock had been ticking, and time had been running out for the boys to revive their favourite group. Yet as the seconds had ticked away, getting closer and closer to the now-or-never moment, the explosive nature of the McBusted bomb that had detonated when the timer hit zero surprised even them. And it wouldn't have happened if Matt, in particular, hadn't kept coming back to the idea – year after year after year. He said jokingly, yet with some sincerity to The Vault, 'If I'm honest, I always thought we would [reunite]. I kept the dream alive!'

James was more circumspect; he had been burned too many times not to be. 'I probably dreamed that we would, but honestly, if you'd asked me before, I would genuinely have said no,' he said to The Vault. 'I didn't want to do something that was going to be really sad. And it can be perceived to be really sad to come back as half a band. The way this whole supergroup happened was amazing; I got so excited about it . . . We did want to do something and the way everything happened naturally with McFly has just been a real blessing for all of us.'

The question on everybody's lips was: what about Charlie? There was no six-foot-something, indie-music-loving model in the line-up; that was plain to see. For so long, he'd blocked the idea of a Busted reunion, and it seemed he still wasn't prepared to join his former bandmates onstage again – but at least their previous animosity had been completely laid to rest. James said at the press conference, 'He's not ready to do this yet. We don't know if he will, but we are good friends. Some people like to make out that we don't get along because it's good drama – but we are actually good friends.' And Matt said to *Daybreak*, 'The door's open [for Charlie]. Maybe hopefully one day . . .'

James added to *Showbiz 411*, 'He's fine with this, he's very supportive; we're supportive of him.' It had been a long time coming, but it seemed there was peace at last.

The papers, however, were full of the story that Charlie had been paid a little sweetener for his share of the Busted name: a little sweetener rumoured to be in the region of six figures. Whatever the facts, he was definitely backing his former band-mates' decision to form McBusted. Charlie publicly tweeted, 'Just wanted to say that though I am not joining @mattjwillis and @jamesbourne on their new venture, I wish them all the very best with it!'

A 'source' told the *Mirror*, 'Charlie wishes the boys lots of luck but he wanted absolutely no involvement . . . All three sat down amicably and worked out a figure that everyone was happy with. Charlie made it clear in no uncertain terms that that's it for him and the boys now, it's finished.'

For McBusted, it was just beginning. And everyone wanted to know how the band had got together – whose idea was it? That was something the boys had a lot of fun with in interviews. On *Daybreak*, Harry was the man. On *5 NewsTalk Live*, it was Dougie. The bassist said blithely, 'It was all my idea, the supergroup. I got everyone together.'

In truth, it was those gigs at the Royal Albert Hall that had cemented it all. Danny told The Vault, 'When we performed at the Albert Hall, we knew there was magic onstage. It was amazing.' It had been such a special occasion that all six friends had instantly thought, This is something we *have* to do. As Matt might have put it via one of his solo songs, it was too incredible a union to let it go to waste. They had to give it life and let it fly. It was Harry who referenced the decade-long bond between the six of them at the press conference, saying, 'We've always got on so well with Matt and James . . . It's our ten-year anniversary – it's a time to celebrate and have fun and we just thought, Why not?'

Going on tour was a prospect they couldn't stop grinning about. Tom said in the press conference, 'You couldn't wipe the smile off our faces. It was the most excited we'd been in ten years.' It felt like everything had fallen into place, so much so that Tom revealed in the VT *McBusted: The Birth* that the tour was 'the obvious thing to do'.

The McBusted tour may have been obvious to Tom – but it turned out Danny was the last to know. He revealed on *Fearne and McBusted*, 'For some reason I was the last to find out about this. For some reason our manager Fletch thought I wouldn't want to do it. I don't know why. When Fletch sat me down on the tour bus, he said, "Just so you know, Danny, I've come to you last because I wanted to check with everybody else. [He paused] I sort of knew that everybody else would be up for doing it. I was worried that you wouldn't really want to do it, that it wouldn't be your thing."

'I was like, "What?!"

'"Going on tour with Busted; you know, joining the two bands."

'I just went, "F**k yeah! That's amazing!" I was so excited.

'And he was like, "Wow. This is amazing. This is *all* going to work, then."'

What had really made it work in the first instance was, of course, James's gig at the Manchester Apollo, which had sparked off the whole idea of the supergroup. And Tom gave credit where it was due. He said magnanimously to The Vault, 'I think the crowd at Manchester that night can take credit.'

The enthusiasm was unstoppable.

The band just hoped, now, that potential ticket buyers would feel the same as they did. To fill eleven arenas would take an awful lot of people, a hell of a lot of fans. It was ambitious. It was pushing it.

Was it all going to fall flat on its face?

It was the band's first night at the O2 Arena in London. Matt was nervous. He kept shaking his whole body, trying to warm himself up, to get himself psyched. The crowd sounded awfully quiet out there.

It was time. He and James, Tom and Harry, Danny and Dougie walked out to greet their audience.

There were only 400 people there.

The band plugged their guitars into the amps. Matt's bass squealed with

Was it all going to fall flat on its face?

feedback. He plucked a note, just to get into it. The sound came only from the onstage amp. *What?*

The main PA system wasn't switched on. Surely some mistake? He glanced, panicked, at their tech guy, but the chap was leaning against the sound desk with his arms crossed, shaking his head. There was no point in turning on the PA for only 400 people.

The guys launched into 'What I Go to School For'. It sounded *rubbish*. Matt's heart sank. He started sweating.

The 400 people came together at the front of the stage, waving their home-made banners forlornly in the vast, empty arena.

Matt swallowed hard. They were going to sink without a trace. McBusted were done for.

He gasped for breath. *Is this what drowning feels like?*

*

Matt Willis started awake, and sat up in bed, his heart racing and his body coated in sweat. Just a nightmare, he told himself. It was only a nightmare.

One that he hoped wouldn't come true when tickets went on sale on Friday.

FIFTEEN

Step by Step

Sitting round a large breakfast table in London, six good friends gathered together to break bread. Usually, a meeting of mates like this would be punctuated with raucous laughter, ribald jokes and smiles as wide as the desert. But on this particular morning, with these particular six friends, their mouths were as dry as dust and there was more nervous tension than toast being handed round the table. An edgy quiet hovered over the group. McBusted were having breakfast – and they were waiting. Waiting, waiting, waiting for news.

No going back now. We're in this together

All of them were nervous about the ticket sales. Had they been too cocky? Yet as James put it to Fearne Cotton – and to his band-mates that morning, 'No going back now. We're in this together.'

He later explained to Fearne the agony of waiting to see if the gigs had sold. 'You really do dangle your balls out there,' he said frankly.

The tickets for the McBusted tour had gone on sale that morning. Fletch had promised them all that he would ring with an update as soon as there was news. But all the band's phones were staying frustratingly silent. They all sat round the table, willing them to ring.

They didn't.

Was this a bad sign, they wondered, or a good one?

At 9.15 a.m. – just fifteen minutes after the ticket hotlines opened – the call came in.

There was a ripple of excitement around the table. Sharp intakes of breath were taken. Sweaty palms were wiped down trouser legs. The phone was lifted; the screen swiped to answer the call.

'Hello?'

Danny remembered it all on The Vault. 'The day that tickets went on sale was such a special day. We were all sat round having breakfast, waiting for our manager to give us the first bit of news. And when it came in . . .

'I actually got a bit emotional. I couldn't believe it – how well the tickets were selling. It was amazing.'

For the tickets weren't just selling well.

They were selling *out*.

Eleven arenas: just like that. More than 140,000 tickets sold in fifteen minutes. Almost 10,000 seats a minute. The tour was completely sold out in just 900 seconds.

As James said to The Vault, 'We were just like, "*What?*"'

McBusted is born: the superband announce the awesome news on *Daybreak* (top) and at their own press conference (bottom), where Busted's debut album artwork is revived to criminally good effect.

No one does a human pyramid like McBusted.

Rocking out: the band show off their sexy sixsome style on *Ant & Dec's Saturday Night Takeaway*.

They might not quite hit 88 m.p.h. in this golf buggy, but McBusted are driving into a very bright future.

James and Tom nail their McBusted jumps as the band play the gig of their career at Hyde Park on 6 July 2014.

As the supergroup play 'Five Colours in Her Hair', a multicoloured rainbow arcs above the stage. Six is the magic number.

Matt spoke about his shock on *5 NewsTalk Live*. 'We can't really comprehend what's just happened. We announced eleven dates and we thought we were being quite optimistic. Eleven arenas, that's quite a big deal. And before we knew it they sold out . . . It's just incredible.'

Tom agreed wholeheartedly with his bandmate. He said to a fan in a YouTube video, 'What we think's been amazing and what we couldn't predict is the fans' reaction to it. The demand is so high. The fans really cared passionately about these guys and Busted and us.'

And people were responding passionately to the supergroup. Even Danny's fiancée Georgia was engaged with the idea. She said on *All Star Mr & Mrs*, 'I was definitely more of a Busted fan – but shh, don't tell Danny.' People had been waiting for so long for a Busted reunion, and that in itself would have been exciting. But this – this was as if someone had suddenly invented time travel. It was pop with the most ding-a-ling bells and wow-inspiring whistles and pumping pyrotechnics that supergroup stardom could buy.

Tom had his own theory as to why it was working so very, very well. He said to The Vault, 'What's awesome about it is it's not something from the past that's coming back and re-forming. It's something new. It's something that's completely not been done yet.'

Also new were the formations the band were rocking on red carpets. The night of the press conference, they'd got straight into the swing of a superband's life by attending the premiere of *The Hunger Games: Catching Fire* together in London's Leicester Square. And as the paparazzi snapped away, eager to get a shot of the new band, McBusted debuted a red-carpet stance that others could only look longingly at.

Oh, yes. The human pyramid.

Matt said on *Sunday Side Up*, 'That was James Bourne's idea. The genius that is James Bourne came up with it. We wanted to do something fun and something a bit different and so we decided to do a human pyramid ... [which was] something fun, but *slightly* rubbish.'

It was like something out of *Transformers*. One moment there were six McBusted-ites standing side by side on the red carpet, the next – *pow!* – pyramid formation. Miley Cyrus could only twerk: *this* was a specialist move that put all other pop stars in the shade – of their enormous triangular shadow. It was on another level, on *three* levels, to be precise.

Forming the base were Danny, Matt and Harry. Next up: the original writing partnership of James and Tom. And crowning the creation, like the decorative prow of a supergroup ship, was Dougie, arm held high in the air.

The band couldn't help enthusing about it on The Vault.

I've never seen a band do a human pyramid

'I've never seen a band do a human pyramid,' commented Danny.

'You need six members in a band to do a human pyramid. Are there any other bands in the UK that can do a human pyramid?' Tom asked his assorted bandmates.

There was a contemplative pause.

Then Matt spoke, 'I don't know of any that have ... not any that thought it was a *good* idea.'

Tom then stated the obvious. 'It took people by surprise. They weren't expecting it.'

They certainly weren't. And, with that in mind, the group seemed determined to come up with a surprising camera-ready formation every time they appeared in public as a group. The *Cosmo* Awards saw them striking a pose with three of the band holding the other three upside down, showing off a fair amount of bare torso as their shirts flipped down, as well as a half-cartwheel dismount that would impress any PE teacher. This wasn't red-carpet posturing: it was a gymnastics display.

The human pyramids and half-cartwheels were indicative of just how much fun they were having together – and they hadn't even started rehearsing yet. As Tom said to the press conference on 11 November, 'What makes [McBusted] different [to cynical reunions or mash-ups] is that there's a genuine relationship between us. There were always blurred lines between McFly and Busted back in the day. Behind the scenes, they were even more blurred. I was nearly in Busted – which I am now! It's taken me ten years, the longest audition process *ever*.'

James chipped in with, 'And if Busted hadn't happened or I wasn't in Busted, I might have been in McFly.'

To which all of McFly immediately murmured, 'Not sure' and 'Don't know about that' – to James's amusement. In the end, he simply settled for the blanket, 'Our musical histories are intertwined.' With which everyone agreed.

The friendships between the boys – and the good-natured ribbing that came with those close relationships – were part of their appeal. No wonder so many people wanted to buy tickets for the tour. McBusted looked as if they were having the best fun ever being a band together: who wouldn't want to join that party?

Asked for his favourite McFly song at the press conference, Matt commanded himself to 'Remember a McFly song, remember a McFly song . . .' to tease the gang – before opting for 'Transylvania', because that's the one his good friend and fellow bassist Dougie sings most on. 'I like that one,' he said to Dougie, giving him an affectionate squeeze. 'I like it 'cause you sing.'

Backstage at the Jingle Bell Ball in Belfast, when asked about the potential tour set list and the bands' respective numbers of hit records, Matt pointed out that Busted had had only two albums, so they had fewer hits, and then joked to McFly, 'Seven number ones over ten years ain't really that good . . .'

And when Matt realised on The Vault that, on *The Big Reunion*, if band members were missing, they were usually just replaced with other people, he joked with Tom and James that, 'We could have maybe got Tom in [to join a Busted-only reunion].' And Tom replied in kind, 'That would have been way better than McBusted – we should have just done that!'

So even the interviews were full of fun. But, as always, what Tom, James, Dougie, Danny, Matt and Harry were really all about was the music. The performance. The live gig.

And their debut TV performance as a unified band would be one to remember, taking place on the night the tickets went on sale, Friday, 15 November 2013. Having filled up on breakfast and the good news of the sell-out tour – to which more dates were being added, as soon as the promoters could confirm them – the gang headed to the BBC studios to perform for Children in Need.

Ten million viewers wasn't too much pressure for their first live TV gig, was it?

Matt would later recall on *Sunday Side Up*, 'I've not been so nervous about a performance ever in my life.'

For Danny, meanwhile, 'It reminded me of when we played our show at the Albert Hall – the excitement we had. We were like little excited kids at Christmas.'

That was plain for all to see. The performance started with just McFly onstage – though there was a small hint of things to come, as Harry had the McBusted logo stamped in red on his white bass drum. McFly were singing 'All About You' – but only for about thirty seconds. As Tom went into the final refrain, the one the band would always pause on before singing the final 'you . . .', he deliberately hesitated as usual – but then the 'Year 3000' intro kicked in, where normally there'd be pursed lips and oohing. The audience knew what was coming. The screams and the raised hands and the crazy jumps started with them even before Matt and James ran on energetically from the side of the stage.

> I've not been so nervous about a performance ever in my life

Danny took great pleasure in making the introductions. 'Ladies and gentlemen, Children in Need, please welcome, for the first time ever, *McBusted*!'

And then they were off. It was a shortened medley of their Albert Hall set list: 'Year 3000', 'Air Hostess' and 'Shine a Light' boiled down to four minutes of magic. The unity within the gang was even more apparent this time. Tom and James, and Dougie and Matt on the other side of the stage, would share one mic for each duo, clearly loving every moment. Matt's freestyled shouts to the crowd had got even more confident and enthused. And the audience responded in kind. Rarely have the BBC studios seen such a reaction. It was more like the mosh pit at the Electric Ballroom in Camden than a charity fundraising programme on straitlaced BBC1. Hands aloft, jumping up and down to match the musicians onstage, everyone was having the time of their lives.

McBusted demonstrated some new moves. As 'Air Hostess' began, and Dougie and Matt did their thing on their basses, the other three guitarists gathered together at the side of the stage and made a new formation to emulate their red-carpet poses. In staggered height order in a crouched position, they pointed with long straight arms towards the bassists. And when the main thrust of the song kicked in, the five of them joined together to debut a high-kicking, high-energy routine.

As ever, though, it was all about the Busted jumps. Dougie and Tom went off on one as the other three took vocals, and as the set came to a close, and a glittering array of silver tickertape rained down on them, the five guitarists gathered round Harry once more for a final, spirited jump to end it all. *Boom.*

A stomping live TV performance. A sell-out arena tour. An incredible 200,000 followers on Twitter for the @mcbusted account in a matter of hours. A 622 per cent combined spike in streams of the bands' music on Spotify.

No wonder Matt said to Children in Need, 'This is probably up there as one of the greatest days of my life.'

*

On 24 November, McFly released a new single, 'Love Is on the Radio'. The supergroup thing had taken on a life of its own – and taken everyone by surprise with its success – but of course McFly were still an existing band with a whole schedule booked in months in advance. The unrelenting machinations behind record releases couldn't grind to a halt that quickly.

The gang did get together to record a special McBusted mix of the new track though. The song had been written by Tom, Danny and James anyway, so it was kind of a McBusted record already – those blurred lines again. Or, as Matt put it on *Sunday Side Up*, 'It's very incestuous.'

The McBusted mix bore all the hallmarks of their previous collaborations. It was a rockier version than the McFly-only one, with the drums and guitars higher in the mix. Matt's punchy voice chiming with Danny's gave it a harder sound than the other – you could hear that Blink-182 inspiration coming through. With five vocalists joining forces, too, the overall impact was a bit more raucous and meaty, and with more layers to the sound.

The McFly single went to number six. They still had it. Another top-ten hit to add to their collection.

'Love Is on the Radio' had more of a country-music vibe to it than had previously been heard from either band. A fiddle and a harmonica were high in the mix. The languorous pace suggested hot summer days in the Deep South, and the 'hey!' that punctuated the song was like a line-dancing enthusiast dipping his hat at the end of a phrase. It was a new sound that James was clearly into. In December he released new music with another new band, called 88 (no prizes for guessing where the name comes from: that sweet-spot speed the DeLorean has to hit in *Back to the Future* in order to time-travel), which he'd formed with the sixty-year-old American musician Eric Bazilian. Their first single was 'Angels Walk Beside You', which began with a harmonica and also had a country-music slant to it, albeit with an electric guitar solo in the middle. It was slower than 'Love Is on the Radio' – a hopeful, yearning, inspirational song, about how there are always friends around you, something James was now appreciating more than ever – but the two songs were stylistically similar.

Eric Bazilian revealed to JamesBourneBrasil.com,

James and I have an amazing connection. Despite the difference in our ages, we are both inspired by the same music, the same sounds, and the same lyrical themes. Things go very quickly when we get together. Usually we write a song in a day. We've got a whole album recorded; at some point we will definitely release it. But, first things first . . . he's got a lot on his plate right now.

The 88 album wasn't the only record with a question mark hanging over its release. McFly's sixth album had been recorded in Texas in the summer, just as they'd planned, with Danny co-producing it along with Jason Perry; and when the McBusted press conference was held in November, the idea was still to release it in spring 2014, on the band's own Super Records label.

Yet, as date after date got added to the McBusted tour, it became clear that the album was going to have to be delayed.

Danny said to Fearne Cotton on *Fearne and McBusted*, 'The McFly album got put on pause. So hard. We were like, "Can we not release our album first?" The promoter offered us a tour so early that we were like, "We've got to do it." Some of the McFly fans weren't really happy with us. It's an incredible album. The album's amazing.'

It was hard. For the Royal Albert Hall gigs, too, had been so well reviewed that, finally, after ten years of hard work and effort, McFly had at long last been recognised as a genuinely talented and important band on the music scene. Journalist Seamus Duff wrote in the *Metro*:

> **Some of the McFly fans weren't really happy with us**

They've toured stadiums, sold out shows, starred in films and reality shows – and yet they seem unfairly overlooked by a lot of media outlets and brushed off as mere 'boy-band pop fodder'. This is incredibly unfair and a disservice to what could arguably be one of the best bands this country has ever produced. ... They are an act who have played their own instruments and written their own material. Notably, they trumped the Beatles when their debut album reached the top of the charts. You could even argue that the two bands are comparable. ... Despite the best McFly songs being better than some of the Beatles' work, Tom, Dougie, Danny and Harry are never given the same credit. ... It's time McFly were celebrated for what they really are: a talented group of musicians and singers, not a dismissible boy band.

But as Danny put it to The Vault, 'Suddenly, this happened. It's all change. Plans are changing all the time.' And so now they were leaving all their success behind to form McBusted; or, perhaps, standing on its shoulders to make something even better – just like a human pyramid in itself.

It was a decision that the band members were embracing fully. Harry said to The Vault, 'McFly is there for us always but . . . it's refreshing [to be doing McBusted].' Dougie agreed in his usual kooky way, comparing being in McFly to eating spaghetti Bolognese for ten years straight in an interview with the entertainment journalist Enas Refaei. For him, it was nice for the band to be tucking into some carbonara for a change (Matt claimed, 'I'm the cream'). Tom even said on 5 NewsTalk Live, 'It is really good. It's much more fun than just being McFly. That was dull and boring in comparison to being in McBusted.' And he added to The Vault, 'It feels like something new. Days when I see in the schedule that it's a McBusted day and not a McFly day, it feels like, "Ah, it's a different day."'

And Tom's days were about to be very different indeed. Shortly before the McBusted press conference, he and Giovanna had announced some very special news via the medium of YouTube. In a charming video, they carved pumpkins to a soundtrack of them singing along to Tom's pink ukulele – and then revealed the message in the lit pumpkins: WE'RE HAVING A BABY. Back in 2001, Hallowe'en for Tom had meant lost dreams. Twelve years later, the traditional glowing pumpkins of the season burned brightly with a new dream that was definitely coming true.

Their baby was due just weeks before the McBusted tour would begin, which was a big talking point in the band's interviews – and an opportunity for Dougie to crack some jokes.

'Where do babies come from?' he asked faux innocently on The Vault.

'I'll show you afterwards,' said Tom.

'Don't show him!' interjected Harry in alarm.

And Harry had a characteristic McFly idea for how YouTube sensation Tom could commemorate the impending happy occasion. Backstage at the Jingle Bell Ball, Harry said to his bandmate, 'What we're requesting now from Tom is a live webcam, and Tom to be there with his ukulele while Giovanna's giving birth and singing a little song about it. Are you down with that?'

Someone Tom could ask for some 'dadvice' about whether or not that was a good idea was of course his new bandmate, Matt, a seasoned father of two. And James for one was certainly full of praise for Matt's fatherly skills. He said on The Vault, 'He does it effortlessly. I don't know how he does it, 'cause it's a big responsibility, two kids, and he just nails it.'

Perhaps he'd honed his skills by looking after James. Matt said to Andi Peters on *Good Morning Britain*, 'Sometimes I do [feel like the daddy of the band]. Literally, every day I have to pick up James. James is the closest to my house. The car comes to get me; then it gets James. Every day I have to get James out of bed. It could be 2.30 in the afternoon, and I still have to get James out of bed. It's like the old days.'

And Matt, despite his light-hearted grumbles about James, was loving the old days being back in his life. Emma said on *Fearne and McBusted*, 'He's like a kid at Christmas. It's like we've had another baby; he's that excited.'

It was an excitement that – just like the Heineken he used to drink – hit spots his other accomplishments somehow couldn't reach. Matt was full of extraordinary news that autumn. First it was revealed that he would appear in the new series of the classic TV sitcom *Birds of a Feather*, playing Garth, the son of leading lady Tracy. The relaunch of the nostalgic favourite attracted close to an astonishing 8 million viewers and was one of the TV hits of the year.

As if that weren't enough, Matt realised a dream most actors never see come true. In his solo interview with The Vault in June 2012, he'd mentioned that he'd quite like to move on from musical theatre and appear in a soap. Eighteen months later, he landed a part on the BBC's top soap, *EastEnders*, playing the boyfriend of Stacey Branning. As James put it in an interview with Enas Refaei, Matt had been busy 'basically making his CV look enormous'.

For some people, those two acting parts alone would, on their own, each be a career highlight. But not for Matt Willis. Music, and being in a band in particular ('I didn't like being solo. I like having people around me,' he once said to the *Daily Record*), had always been his thing. He confided to Enas Refaei, 'Whatever I've done in life, I've always had at the back of my mind: I really want to do Busted music. It was really unsettled, unfinished business for me.' He said frankly in a fan's YouTube video that he 'regretted that decision' to end Busted when they did. He added to The Vault, 'What was so weird about the timing [of McBusted] is that I'd started to think to myself, If we're ever going to do this, we need to do it soon. Then – all of a sudden – *bang*!'

> **Whatever I've done in life, I've always had at the back of my mind: I really want to do Busted music. It was unfinished business for me**

He was aware of the irony of suddenly having to juggle a successful acting career with his passion though. He joked to Enas Refaei, 'And now I've got to ruin everything by being in a pop band again.'

It was weird for James, too. He was having to manage McBusted commitments along with his new musical, *Murder at the Gates*, and his other projects. Though, echoing Matt, he said firmly to *Daybreak*, 'It's been fun [writing musicals] – but it's good to be back in a band.'

With James having lived in America for the past six years or so, however, there were some adjustments to be made. He said to The Vault, 'People in my life [knew me only] when I wasn't in a band, and people are like, "What's happened? Where are you? Where did you go?" Because they're all in another country and they don't understand what it was like the first time here. They're like, "Where have you gone, James?"'

Where he'd gone was to follow his heart. And he was about to follow it all the way to Cornwall, where the band had plans. Great plans.

To make new music.

SIXTEEN

That Thing You Do

In early 2014, there was a knock on the door of James's house in Cornwall. James, hearing it, made his way over to answer it.

He was thirty years old, and currently in a band called McBusted. He wrote songs – and dreamed of the day when he could perform them to millions. Maybe, just maybe, the people who had knocked on his door would be the answer to his prayers.

He pulled open the door.

'Come in,' said James, and he opened the door wide – to welcome his five bandmates home.

He led them through to the living room with its stunning sea view, all of them lugging various bits of equipment and a selection of instruments. Just as in James's parents' house in Southend back in the day, they were going to set up a home recording studio in the living room . . .

... to see what musical magic they might be able to conjure up. Matt for one was delighted to be back in Cornwall. He said to the *West Briton*, 'During the madness of Busted I escaped to Cornwall with James. We basically lived on the beach and "met" lots of girls. So I have very fond memories of Cornwall.'

There were no girls allowed on this writing trip, though. It was strictly business, and boys only. And, amid the windswept winter beaches, they found inspiration to write. Teasingly, they revealed the title of only one track when they appeared on *The Jonathan Ross Show* a few weeks after their trip. Its name? 'OMFG'.

Matt said of his Busted days to The Vault, 'We were never one of those bands that was like, "Oh my God, look how huge we are." We were constantly like, "You're only as good as your next song." We were constantly trying to get better and better.'

And McBusted took that same sentiment – and modesty – into their songwriting sessions. They were coy about what might happen to the music they were making. At the original press con-

> ## We were never one of those bands that was like, 'Oh my God, look how huge we are'

ference, Tom had said, 'For now [McBusted is] just the tour.' But he added, 'I think if we come up with something awesome and we write some songs we think are incredible, then we'd love to release it.' He added to The Vault, 'The tour took us by surprise. If people want us to make music together ... We've been writing songs together for ten years so we never stopped doing that – so I think we could definitely see ourselves doing that.'

The idea of a McBusted commercial release wasn't what drove them, though. As Harry said to a fan in a YouTube video, 'Even if we weren't planning on doing an album, writing would happen anyway.' And James agreed: 'We're writing partners, with or without the band.' He went further on *McBusted: The Birth*: 'We make music together; we've always written together. It's real. There's a real relationship there. And so, when the idea of forming this supergroup came about, that was when I knew: this is the right way to do this.'

And the supergroup were looking as if they were definitely going to have a life beyond the massive thirty-five arenas they'd sold out for the spring – and not simply because that accomplishment alone was one of the most successful music events in recent history. Tom said with confidence to *5 NewsTalk Live*, 'I think we could definitely get excited about writing some new McBusted songs.'

And it seemed that excitement was one of the things they unpacked with their kit in James's front room in Cornwall. Matt revealed to Jonathan Ross, 'We always said that we weren't going to *say* we were going to bring out music, because we didn't want to go away and make music and it be terrible.

'But we went away, we did some writing – and it wasn't terrible.'

That would literally be music to their fans' ears. As to what the McBusted sound would be like, fans could make an educated guess. James confided on *Fearne and McBusted*, 'We're experimenting. We don't know exactly how it's going to be, but we thought, No harm in seeing what happens.' As writing partners over a decade in the making, it was likely to be pretty special.

Guitars would definitely feature. McFly's output of late had been very happy, summery pop – perhaps a sign of the loved-up status of the group, with Harry, Danny and Tom all married, or about to be. With Matt happily married and James still with Gabriela (he said to The Vault, 'We've been together for a while. And we're having a really good time'), perhaps happiness would be the order of the day.

And Dougie could contribute on that front, too. Before Christmas, pictures had started circulating of him hanging out with fellow pop star Ellie Goulding. Every interview McBusted gave included an awkward moment when the presenter would knowingly ask Dougie if he had anything to share. The rest of the band would fall silent – the quiet bond of brothers in arms – but with mischievous smirks written plainly across their faces, as Dougie innocently denied he had anything to talk about on the romance front.

> **Dougie innocently denied he had anything to talk about on the romance front**

Yet, as the winter blossomed into spring, their relationship blossomed, too, and he and Ellie finally confessed publicly that they were dating. Dougie said to Fearne Cotton, 'All is good in that area. All is very, very good.' Meanwhile, Ellie said sweetly on *Alan Carr: Chatty Man*, 'He is lovely,' and raved to *Self* magazine, 'Love is beyond everything, beyond the universe . . . I've definitely met someone.'

It seemed McBusted would retain their sense of fun and humour in the new material, though, despite their grown-up married status.

Matt later said to the *Daily Record*, 'I was with Dougie last night and we were writing an appreciation song about boobs.' He added, with all the experience borne of ten years in the music business, 'But we can't just write an album of songs about boobs.'

For now, though, the album had to take a backseat to the tour. The first sell-out arena was booked for 17 April at Glasgow's SSE Arena. And there was a lot of work to be done before they were ready to wow their fans – not least, deciding on the set list.

Danny said confidently on The Vault, 'There's fourteen number ones between us – so that's the set list, done.' Dougie came up with a typically crazy plan to *Chronicle Live*, 'The only word to describe this set list is going to be "gigantor". Maybe we should just blur all the tunes together into one two-hour song . . .' And it was clear everyone had their favourites. Danny and Matt both loved 'Air Hostess', while Dougie went for 'Who's David?' – to James's approval ('I'm most excited about that one, that's my favourite song,' he enthused at a McBusted press conference). That press conference itself was the scene of a veritable on-location brainstorm.

Harry kicked things off by saying, 'I was a massive fan of Busted. So the first thing I thought [about the tour] was, Awesome – we get to play Busted songs.

'I'm sick of McFly songs. I love "Over Now" and "Better Than This", so we'll play those two, please, if that's cool with you guys. We get to choose one each for sure that we get to play, so I'll take . . . "Over Now".'

Tom was too excited to choose. 'I'm looking forward to playing all of them.' Though he then added, 'I like playing "Year 3000". When we did that at the Albert Hall, that was amazing. When that intro starts . . . That was really cool.'

Danny, swept away in the moment, then named a little-known special-edition Busted track, 'When Day Turns Into Night'. Responding to the blank faces of the press arrayed before them, the rest of the band all spoke up: 'All the hits!', 'Erase that . . .'

To Magic FM, Danny explained that, in actual fact, the selection process would be 'exactly what we would do if we were just doing a tour [as McFly]. Which songs have the fans not heard for a while? Let's play that one, that one, that one.' And Tom chipped in, 'We didn't want it to be like, "OK, we're McFly and Busted so we have to play half and half." We just want it to feel like, "We are a band now, the six of us, these are all of our songs together . . . How do we make the most awesome set list? Regardless of what song is whose: what makes the best set list?"'

While the press were keen to pin them down on which tracks fans were going to hear at the gigs, the band were keeping shtum, waiting for the big reveal in Glasgow. At yet another press conference, Dougie, displaying his unique talent for similes, said firmly, 'We don't want to commit. It's like New Year. You don't want to say what you're doing until the last minute.' And James simply commented, 'We want to make sure we love what we do.'

There was little chance they'd do anything but love it. Harry confided to the press, 'I personally can't wait to play the Busted tunes. I was in the rehearsal room the other day on my own, cheekily listening to "Sleeping with the Light On", playing along, going, "I can't wait for this!"'

That was one track that might need a bit more work, though. 'We had a singalong of "Sleeping with the Light On" at my house the other night,' Tom revealed at a press conference. 'James was trying to get us to do all the harmonies – and failing miserably.'

Harry summed it all up to The Vault: 'I'm sure we'll all go to rehearsals with different ideas and kind of bring it together and we'll see.'

And scheduled in among those rehearsals were more media appearances. There were Danny and Matt on *Sunday Side Up*, gamely attempting the iconic Busted jump in a navy twinsie. There was the inevitable chat-show appearance on *The Jonathan Ross Show* – the sofa only just big enough to hold the sextet (James perched nimbly on the arm). And then Matt and Dougie were reunited with *I'm a Celebrity* hosts Ant and Dec on *Ant & Dec's Saturday Night Takeaway*, where the band staged a sing-off with newly formed rock group 'McDonnelly': Ant and Dec sporting comedy rock-star wigs. Matt was clearly getting back into the swing of his role in McBusted: for the TV appearance, his head was shaved and the remainder of his dark hair fashioned back into the beginnings of a Mohawk.

It was an interesting look for the school run for the father-of-two. But, as his wife revealed to Fearne Cotton, Matt was taking his new pop-star responsibilities very seriously. 'Listen,' he'd said to Emma. 'You've got to stop thinking of me as Matt. I am Matt at home, but in the band I am Matt from Busted.' And that definitely required a new haircut.

The rest of Matt's look was defined by his array of brightly coloured tattoos, including a tribute to his daughter, whom he nicknamed 'Wizz', which he had across his ribs, and two full sleeves of artwork down his arms. He told Steve Wright on his radio show, 'I started [my tattoos] when I was twenty-one and I thought I was going to be in a pop band for the rest of my life – so I smothered myself in very uncastable tattoos.' He gave the back story to FleckingRecords.co.uk: 'I was in New Zealand and I got a really crappy tattoo on my wrist, so I went to get it covered . . . and I got a bit carried away. I'm totally addicted to tattoos, man, I want as many as I can get.'

And he'd found kindred spirits in his new bandmates. McFly were already tattoo enthusiasts: they'd got into 'band' tattoos in a big way, in the form of each of them taking a letter to spell out 'YMCA', so the word was whole when they were together; and they'd also got their famous 'foot' tattoos back when they were promoting *Just My Luck* in America. Dougie had 'Athlete's', Tom 'Big', Harry 'Bare', and Danny 'Good Ef'. With Matt now in the gang, and the fun-spirited musicians always game for a laugh, a new version of roulette was born.

Tattoo roulette.

Six pieces of paper in a hat. Four labelled 'No'. Two labelled 'Oh Shit'. The climax to the game: the 'Oh Shit' recipients stage a best-of-three bout of rock, paper, scissors in the tattoo parlour, with the loser having to get a design of the others' choosing.

With drugs and drink now off the menu for the supergroup, it was adrenaline-pumping stuff. Tom lost the first round, and ended up with – what else could it be? – the logo of the new group painted indelibly on his foot. He tweeted, 'I lost tattoo roulette . . . I've got the world's worst band name on my foot . . . forever.' Matt did confide that they were coming round to the name now, though, saying to the *Mirror*, 'We've gone through regretting it, and now we embrace it. We think actually, it's so shit, we quite like it!'

And Matt would soon have to get used to liking shit things – for he lost round two of the tattoo game, and his leg became the blank canvas for a little green frog tattoo, in honour of James, whose nickname from the group was 'Frogs'. 'I'm flattered,' laughed his bandmate, clearly tickled at Matt's fate.

Tattoo roulette was only the beginning for the band when it came to high jinks. All of them were looking forward to the craziness of being on tour. Matt said to *5 NewsTalk Live*, 'I think at the core of us we're still reckless and as rock-and-roll as we always were.' Danny cheekily said to heatworld.com, 'We always cause mischief everywhere we go.' And the band were quoted in the *Bolton News* as describing themselves as 'not a band but a gang'.

Matt and Dougie took things even further with their, ahem, special description of the supergroup, with Matt saying to the *Yahoo! Celebrity* website, 'It's like sex with one person – great – sex with two people – now you're talking! Sex with SIX people? That's what this is!'

Dougie coined a new phrase in response: 'McBusted is a sixsome – sex with six people!'

But, all joking aside, things on the road would be a little different from the old days. It was three years since Dougie had gone to rehab; six years since Matt had been clean. Matt said honestly to the *Daily Record*, 'I have flashbacks to drugs every single day – but I know it's some sort of romanticism about the past. You know that it's the past for a very good reason, and I'm constantly reminded of that every time I wake up.'

McBusted is a sixsome; sex with six people!

And for three members of the band, their new sobriety would lead to a very different experience of being onstage while on tour.

Matt was open about the fact that he had spent most of Busted's heyday in a booze-fuelled fog; he always used to get wasted before going onstage. No wonder James said to heatworld.com, 'I think it would be fun to actually sound good this time.'

It was an ambition Matt was aware – and supportive – of. He agreed with his bandmate: 'I just want to put on a really good show. And unfortunately being rock-and-roll doesn't really help you put on a good show.' Danny added, tongue only slightly in cheek, 'We look at ourselves like athletes now.'

For Harry, too, things were different. Since he'd had his epiphany about alcohol and quit drinking completely, his pre-gig warm-ups no longer included a cheeky shot of Dutch courage to send him on his way. He confessed to Fearne Cotton, 'In the past my preparation for going onstage was to drink. Sometimes I'd be like, "Whoa" – and here he mimed waving his drumsticks wildly in the air – "bit too drunk." But now there's me and Dougie ordering herbal teas. Me and Matt comparing workouts. It's good. I'm happy.'

The bromance between Matt and Harry bonding over their workouts was crystal clear. Harry raved chummily to Matt in a McBusted vodcast, 'That's the best thing about you joining: I've got someone to work out with.'

And the workouts weren't the only change. On this tour, the band joked that their rider included camomile and green tea. As Matt put it to *Good Morning Britain*, 'Hard-core.' And, thankful as they were when a fan sent them a flux capacitor cake, Matt and Tom kindly requested in an interview with *London Live* that, next time, a wheat- and gluten-free version would be appreciated. This was rock and roll – the McBusted way.

As the calendar pages were ripped off the wall, one by one, the first date of the tour grew ever closer. The band were rehearsing hard, sorting out new musical arrangements for the tracks, figuring out how to make five guitars playing all at once sound good and – most importantly – dividing up Charlie's lines in the Busted songs.

In a press conference, Harry had said, 'We felt four McFlys made up for one Charlie.'

But Danny was quick to interrupt him: 'Woah, woah, woah – I'm Charlie!'

Matt was even quicker on the uptake: 'And you're twice the man he was!'

In truth, Danny's rock voice would fit in perfectly with the numbers. And Tom was looking forward to singing, too. He said to Magic FM, '[I'll be singing] songs that I've written for Busted that I've never been able to perform before . . . really good fun.'

And fun was, in the end, what it was all about. The band had loads of bright ideas as to how they could make these the most awesome shows ever; they mostly seemed to involve high volume and high explosives. James said to *McBusted: The Birth*, 'We've been given an opportunity to put on a special show and that's what we're going to do.' And Tom concluded, 'I know it's going to be really special – and a hell of a lot of fun.'

By the time Danny spoke to the *Somerset News*, some of the plans were a bit clearer. He said, 'We know we want to blow stuff up and do some crazy stuff. Our philosophy is, no matter what it costs, we put on the best show ever, and we want to put on an amazing show.'

We know we want to blow stuff up

And their fans had enabled them to put on the most amazing show of their entire career. The band were completely gobsmacked at the huge numbers of ticket sales, and the passion with which the idea of the supergroup had been received. Danny shook his head disbelievingly as he said on The Vault, 'It's mental, absolutely mental.'

The tour was bigger than anything either band had ever achieved before, despite all their success and the Guinness world records they'd received for their sell-out tours. Even though both McFly and Busted had enjoyed individual spells as Britain's most popular band, McBusted put them on a whole new level. It was mind-boggling – and somewhat humbling. James put it beautifully on McBusted's YouTube channel: 'They're going to be the biggest shows of our career. For that to happen to all of us, ten years since we started, it's been an unbelievable journey.'

He said simply to Fearne Cotton, 'It meant so much to all of us.'

And Tom explained to Fearne exactly what the fans' support had enabled the band to do. 'Normally on a tour,' he said, 'we'll have loads of ideas and be able to do one of them. But because this tour's so big . . . we literally had a wishlist of stuff we wanted to do and when we sat down for our first meeting we were like, "Great, let's just do all of them."' No wonder he said of his bandmates to *Chronicle Live*, 'James and Matt are going to be like animals uncaged for the first time in ten years.'

But, before the wildness of the former Busted boys could be unleashed on the world, there was one rather significant event in McBusted Land: the birth of Tom and Giovanna's baby. At 7 p.m. on 13 March 2014, the McBusted clan welcomed its newest member. Giovanna tweeted about the happy occasion: 'So in love with our gorgeous little boy Buzz Michelangelo Fletcher.'

And what better way to mark the occasion than with a new YouTube video? No, not the one Harry had suggested. Instead, the Fletchers revealed that, for the past nine months, they'd been working on a time-lapse video of Giovanna's pregnancy, showing every day of her changing body, which played on the screen while Tom sang along with his guitar. They called it 'From Bump to Buzz' and it soon hit nearly 10 million views.

Buzz had timed his arrival well.

Thirty-five days later, his dad and his new 'uncles' prepared to open the biggest tour of their lives.

SEVENTEEN

The Heart Never Lies

They could hear the screams from backstage – and they hadn't even started yet. McBusted gathered in a circle in their dressing room. One dressing room for the six of them. It was a tight squeeze for the sextet, but, as Matt said to *Good Morning Britain*, 'I wouldn't want it any other way.'

James led the group together in a unified, single clap, all twelve hands pressed together simultaneously, not a whisper of a second apart, to ensure that the band were all on the same wavelength for the show ahead. Then the circle broke up. The band members bumped fists as they made their way towards the stage, wishing each other the best broken legs on the planet.

Tom, Dougie and Danny took their places beneath the stage, their guitars ready in their hands. Harry sat behind his drum kit, poised and in position. The four McFly boys had done this so many times before. But this time everything felt different. Six was the magic number.

For James, it was an incredible moment. He had said to Fearne Cotton on *Fearne and McBusted*, about that final Busted Wembley gig so many years before, 'I didn't know that the last show we played at Wembley . . . I didn't know that was our last show. In my mind there was never a last gig. One day, it was over.'

In the next thirty seconds, it would be beginning all over again.

He and Matt looked at each other. This was it. What a journey they'd had, from that first jamming session in Southend-on-Sea to this moment. They'd ridden the wave of Busted's success the first time, and had crashed and burned. Now, like phoenixes, they were rising again, once more preparing to play for thousands upon thousands of people. Matt swallowed hard. It was different without the drink inside him. But, somehow, it was so much more exciting second time around.

Out in the arena, the lights faded to black. The audience shrieked in anticipation.

Out in the arena, the lights faded to black. The audience shrieked in anticipation

And the arena screens flickered into life.

A single date in white on black.

January 14th, 2005.

Roll VT.

Amid a cacophony of calls from the waiting journalists and a blizzard of camera flashes, the three men hurriedly made their way from the room, having just delivered the worst news of two of their young lives.

The door closed behind them. For the first time in three years, there was only silence. How to find the words to say goodbye?

They didn't even try. Matt and James made their way, glumly, to the car park. It was grey concrete all around, as gloomy and as hard and unforgiving as the choices now before them. They faced each other, the end of everything written in the slope of their downturned necks, in their downcast eyes.

They shook hands, formally, but almost immediately Matt flicked his long dark fringe – styled just on the one side in the emo fashion – out of his eyeliner-ringed eyes and pulled James into a massive hug. This wasn't the time for being cool.

This was the end.

James hugged him back, hard. He'd never thought it would finish like this. He pulled his baseball cap down firmly over his eyes, and slipped silently into the waiting car. The door slammed, echoing around the cavernous car park, and the car drove off. Matt couldn't even bear to watch the tail-lights fade away.

Which was why he was so surprised when he heard James call his name at the top of his voice.

'*Matt!*'

His bandmate ran up to him, the car in which he was supposed to be sitting somehow still in sight in the distance, travelling at speed – and yet James was very much here, now, panting and desperate, and clutching a tour programme in his hand. Matt struggled to compute what he was seeing, his forehead furrowed with the effort. James grabbed him and held his arms tight.

'We've got to go back!' he declared vehemently.

'Back?' echoed Matt. 'Back where?'

James paused for a moment – and then delivered the line to end all lines.

'Back . . . to the future!'

Cue screams in the Glasgow SSE Arena on Thursday, 17 April 2014. And cue action. As the video reached its conclusion, Matt and James strapped themselves into the car onscreen, ready for the ride of their lives. James floored the accelerator. The screens flashed to white – and, with that, suddenly, the stage came blazingly to life, with bursts of flame that practically singed the screaming fans in the front row, and with blitzes of blinding lights, dry ice and classic sci-fi lightning strikes. To the awesome sound of the theme tune from *Back to the Future*, the ungodly sight of a flying DeLorean took centre stage.

The fans knew what was coming. They screamed and screamed and screamed for the Second Coming of Matt Willis and James Bourne. The iconic winged doors of the DeLorean lifted, and, simultaneously, Matt and James stepped out of the car. The arena erupted in a volcanic hail of helpless shrieks. As James and Matt strapped on their guitars, the stage was lit once more by a brilliant shower of sparks –

> **James floored the accelerator and suddenly the stage came blazingly to life**

and Tom, Danny and Dougie were launched at stratospheric speed from beneath the stage to land, perfectly in time, ready for the start of 'Air Hostess'. As entrances go, it was – without a doubt – spectacular in every sense of the word.

Matt and Dougie started the bass line, Harry pounded his

drums – and they were off. All six of them were like rockets packed with plutonium fuel, as the five guitarists zoomed round the stage, high-kicking to the moon, and singing their hearts out. Fans didn't know where to look first, there was so much glorious action happening onstage. Tom and James jamming in the corner. Matt creeping up behind Danny so they could Busted-jump in unison. Dougie locking eyes with Harry as they kept the rhythm pounding through the heart of the song. The energy was nuclear. Danny, centre stage, holding court like Springsteen, simply couldn't wipe the smile from his face. The genuine friendship between the group was as transparent to the audience as if they'd had the superpower of X-ray vision. The crowd just wanted to eat them up with a very big spoon, one tasty musician at a time.

As the song reached its triumphant conclusion, Matt raised his bass like a shotgun, playing it above his head. The gang shot straight into the next number: 'You Said No'. It. Sounded. So. Cool. Fans, who hadn't heard these songs played live for a decade, went absolutely nuts. These were the songs they had grown up with; songs that, for the past ten years, had accompanied them in their bedrooms on their stereos, or walking down the street on an iPod. Even with the best speakers in the world, the sound would be small, tinny, tiny and low. Now, the songs' own creators were playing them live, at visceral high volume, on five guitars and a top-of-the-range drum kit. This was more than exciting. This was memory come to life and standing solidly in front of you, taking you by the hand and twirling you around the dance floor at 500 million miles an hour.

Hit after hit, song after song. The secret set list was exposed track by track – and it didn't disappoint. 'Britney', 'Who's David?',

'5 Colours in Her Hair', 'Obviously' . . . No wonder James had said to *Chronicle Live*, 'I'm going to frame this set list after the tour. It's just going to be so good.'

The band made full use of their very expensive set. There were about a hundred lighting changes per song, with big round lights set up on the speakers at the back of the stage, which throbbed in time with the music. The main stage had a circular walkway attached to it – the fans caught in the middle of the circle were ticket holders for the exclusive 'OMFG!' zone – and Tom, Dougie, Danny, Matt and James loved running round it and playing to fans further out in the crowd.

After 'Obviously' came a very special moment. While the others ran off to get a quick drink of water or to towel off the sweat, the lights dimmed, and James was left on his own at the front of the circular walkway, as close as he could get to the very heart of the arena. He had his acoustic guitar in his arms. He started strumming, slowly, the ballad pace of 'Sleeping with the Light On' – the first song he and Matt ever co-wrote. It was just him, his guitar – and 13,000 fans. It was a moment that echoed his life-changing performance at the Manchester Apollo. The thousands of fans sang along with him, word perfect. And James was lit not only by the single spotlight, but by the soft blue lights of the smartphones surrounding him, twinkling like fireflies on the best summer night of your life. As the chorus built, his bandmates returned, harmonising to gorgeous effect.

The next rabbit out of their very big McBusted hat was a UFO. Yes, an all-lights-flashing, jeepers-creepers 3D flying saucer was unleashed on the people of Glasgow. The 'second stage' descended from the ceiling of the arena to showcase Harry in the middle of the 'saucer' on his drums and his five bandmates surrounding him, each with a light-up guitar in neon colours. What else could they play on a UFO but 'Star Girl'?

Busted's track 'Nerdy' followed, then McFly's 'Room on the 3rd Floor' – a song they could all connect with, with their shared history of the InterContinental. And then it was back to the main stage, for 'Thunderbirds Are Go' and a very, very special cover.

There hadn't been much discussion as to which icon they might choose to honour with a cover song. For James, there could be only one answer: Michael Jackson. The artist who had started it all for him, way back when.

And this wasn't just a musical homage – oh no. As the unmistakeable intro of the Jackson 5's 'I Want You Back' resonated around the arena, Danny, James and Matt revealed that it would be a dancing tribute, too. While Dougie and Tom played their guitars like two beautiful bookends, the centre stage was dominated by a dance routine by the other three guitarists – to the delight of fans. McBusted weren't a boy band, but they proved they could groove it with the best of them. James took the lead vocal of his icon; it must have been one of the greatest moments of his life.

It must have been one of the greatest moments of his life

They were getting near the end now, but you wouldn't have known it from their unstoppable energy. They bantered with the crowd, fired merchandise at them from massive T-shirt guns, admired the drag air-hostess outfits some male fans had turned up in, and effected so many effervescent, synchronised Busted jumps it was incredible the stage was still standing. Now they were singing 'Shine a Light'. Now 'What I Go to School For'. Now it was the end.

But, like the Busted story itself, it wasn't. The encore was introduced by another VT. As the video of Tom Fletcher's famous wedding speech rolled, it was interrupted by some very vocal, ahem, wedding crashers. And as, onscreen, Matt swooped behind the top table to rugby-tackle Tom to the floor, the arena rang with the cacophonous chords of 'Crashed the Wedding'. The band were back – and Matt was reprising his original video role as the blushing bride, sporting a gorgeous white wedding gown. Dougie leaped on to his bandmate's back as the bride kept playing 'her' guitar, before both tumbled to the floor in fits of giggles.

Next, they segued into the simple tune of 'All About You', which simply soared, with all six of them chiming in on the vocals.

And there could be only one song to end it all. The song that had set the ball rolling in Manchester. The song that had started their very first set together at the Royal Albert Hall. As three inflatable boobies unfurled above the stage, in tribute to the lyric, McBusted played 'Year 3000', and the Glasgow arena partied as if it were 1999.

To the appreciative roar of the crowd, McBusted left the stage one by one, hurling themselves from a runway of a stage into the air – to land on a crash mat offstage. Each death-defying jump was made to the accompaniment of Harry's dramatic drum rolls, until the drummer himself made his own leap of faith into the dark. On the screens, three words were lit in the fiery typeface of the *Back to the Future* logo:

TO BE CONTINUED . . .

It was a night neither the band nor the audience would ever forget. Harry said to Fearne Cotton afterwards, 'The first night was insane.'

And they still had another thirty-odd gigs to go.

Almost at once, it seemed, the band settled into life on tour. They were receiving rave reviews from the media. POP CONGLOMERATE MORE THAN THE SUM OF THEIR PARTS, championed the *Guardian*; RELENTLESS FUN, screamed the *Telegraph*, pointing out that 'every song had expertly placed pauses for everyone to jump in the air in unison.' And the *Guardian* concluded by saying what everyone was thinking: 'Tonight's trip back in time has conjured an unexpectedly bright future.'

The band celebrated in a slightly more sedate way than in their former hellraising days. Matt revealed to the *Mirror* after the first Glasgow gig: 'Last night I got back to the hotel and we had sandwiches and nachos, and a mint tea. I was like, f**k dude, this is not the way we used to do things.' But he added, 'We're all older and not quite so chaotic as we once were – but it still feels like that vibe; it's still troublesome.'

And they took that troublesome vibe with them on the tour bus, as the six got used to life on the road. Matt confessed on *Fearne and McBusted*, 'I've been out loads on this tour, which I thought we wouldn't do. Dougie and I have started smoking cigars.' Harry attributed that to 'Dougie's bad influence' on a McBusted vodcast, but Tom perhaps had it right when he said, 'I think you're bad influences on each other.'

James was quickly singled out for being the sleepiest boy on the bus, later winning the title of 'Sleepy Sleeperson, Best Sleeper' in a McBusted vodcast. But he was active on the McBusted Twitter account at least, which was full of pranks and jokes detailing the band's backstage shenanigans. Here was James posting a Vine of Harry 'pumping iron' – as the former *Strictly* winner lifted the domestic appliance up and down.

James and Matt found themselves impressed by how McFly had matured since they'd last toured together, all those years ago. With a decade's experience under their belts, and with the confidence that comes of being a headlining act, Tom, Danny, Dougie and Harry were at the top of their game – and assertive with it. James said on a McBusted vodcast, 'Back in the olden days, I feel like we were quite polite; I felt like I would never really say much [e.g. to the crew]. If something wasn't quite right, I wouldn't say something . . . You [guys] stand up for yourself [now].' And Matt agreed. Impressed by his bandmates, he dubbed them 'seasoned pros'.

The biggest beef backstage was about the windiness of the McFly boys, though. While the four of them had, for ten years, been quite comfortably farting in each other's company, the Busted boys found it quite a culture shock. Danny's fiancée Georgia did say of her beloved on *All Star Mr & Mrs*, 'I mean, he farts more than not. I mean it's constant' – so it seemed it was something Matt and James would have to get used to. Matt, who had discovered the charms of various vitamins and health supplements since giving up drink, tried to tackle the issue by supplying 'digestive enzymes' to his bandmates. They did stop the farts – but just transferred the gas from one end to the other.

For McFly, the biggest adjustment was to James's personal hygiene – or lack thereof. Harry said diplomatically to the radio station Fun Kids, 'James is a very unique character. He's amazing to be in a band with because he's very funny and he's very unique – hence why he's such a creative person.' Yet the creativity came with other issues attached. Harry revealed, 'James Bourne is basically a tramp-slash-pop star. He's proud to say he's never bought a can of deodorant in his life. He wears the same outfit for two weeks. Showers every four days.'

Which meant he wasn't involved when the rest of McBusted had a naked communal shower after the Sheffield show!

Each member of the band had his own favourite moments in the show itself. Tom said sincerely to James on the McBusted vodcast that, for him, his highlight was, 'Watching you go out [to sing "Sleeping with the Light On"]; I really like that. That whole little moment.' For Danny, hilariously, it was the end. But he explained, 'Jumping into the crash mat at the end [is my favourite bit] – because you feel like you've done an amazing show and you get to launch yourself on a crash mat. It's the best way to get offstage ever.'

When McBusted had a naked communal shower

Matt, typically, was always striving to see how they could improve things. In response to Danny's comment, he said thoughtfully, 'It would be better if one of us could do a backflip.'

Matt had noticed there was something different about the fans this time round. He told the *Mirror*, 'There was a bra thrown [last night] – it was quite a big bra, though. When we were in Busted, the bras were quite small. She's grown up! They aren't sports bras or training bras anymore.'

The show was evolving all the time, too. Dougie introduced a helium-voiced solo for himself. Sometimes it was 'My Heart Will Go On' from *Titanic*; Harry would join him to play Leo to Dougie's Kate, Dougie's arms splayed dramatically out to his sides as Harry held him close in a tight embrace. At other times, he'd perform 'Wonderwall', in tribute to the Gallagher brothers. He didn't sound quite like Danny and Matt had done when they were singing Oasis songs in pubs, back before they made it big – but he was just as entertaining.

The band started using the gigs to showcase some of their other skills, too. Danny was known to throw in a burst of opera vocal from his time on *Popstar to Operastar*. Harry borrowed Danny's guitar to demonstrate his multi-instrument musicianship. A childlike, staccato version of 'Good King Wenceslas' followed.

It's the most fun I've had onstage – ever

Matt rocked out some of his old moves from his days of West End glory in *Wicked*. And – in a classic, true McBusted moment – Tom and James took a trip down memory lane by giving a short performance of 'Consider Yourself', complete with dance routine, in a nod to the role they had shared as child stars: that of Master Oliver Twist. The band also, perhaps predictably, took to forming their famed human pyramid each night too.

For James, his opinion of the show was quite simple. He said on the vodcast, 'It's the most fun I've had onstage – ever.'

And that was all to do with the people he was performing with. Matt revealed to *Good Morning Britain*, 'What you see onstage is what it's like. This isn't two different groups of people that you've just shoved together and said, "Right, do this": this is six mates who went, "How about we just do something awesome together?"'

James agreed. He said to *Chronicle Live*, 'The relationship between our two bands is unique. I was trying to think of any other bands who could do this [supergroup thing] where it would actually work. It's really rare. We've all been friends for so many years.'

Harry added to The Vault, 'For bands [in themselves] to get on these days is rare. For a band to stay together for ten years is rare. And to have two other new guys come along and for us all to get on equally as well – it's awesome.'

Dougie summed it up in *McBusted: The Birth*, 'We've got two more best friends onstage with us.'

And Danny joined the love-in. Speaking to the *Somerset News*, he said, 'The friendship between us is second-to-none. It's a connection on a different level. We never try and "be" anything. It's six lads who're all good mates. There's lots of energy and we all want to not only perform, but hang out together. It's just a really good vibe.'

There was only one cloud on McBusted's sunny horizon. During the tour, James and Gabriela called time on their relationship. Gabby tweeted on 5 June 2014, 'I'm sure some of you already figured it out, but after almost eight years, James and I are no longer together. It was fun while it lasted.' The long distance between the couple couldn't have helped, but there were earlier signs that perhaps it wasn't a relationship that was going to endure. When James was asked by The Vault about his marriage plans in December, he'd replied awkwardly, 'I'm not quite ready for that yet.'

What he was ready for, though, was the wicked wave of career resurgence that he was currently riding. Just weeks after Gabby's tweet, McBusted took on a huge gig when they supported the mammoth boy band One Direction at their Paris stadium gig on 21 June. They knew the band themselves well, with Danny, Dougie and Tom having worked with the 1D boys on all three of their albums. And it was a relationship that was still thriving, as Danny told Fearne Cotton: 'Niall was over the other night writing. They're really nice guys. We got a really good song.'

Niall Horan and the other 1D lads were over the moon at the idea of McBusted supporting them. For many of them, their first ever gig had been that now-historic joint Busted–McFly arena tour back in 2004 – a whole decade ago, as Tom was keen to point out to a fan on a YouTube video: 'We couldn't have planned [McBusted] any better. It's almost ten years to the day since we went on tour with these guys, and now we're going on tour again.'

Niall tweeted his excitement: "F**kkkk yeeaaaahhhh! Tomorrow is the day! @mcbusted are playing at our show! Aaaaggghhh! Soo excited!' He wasn't the only celebrity fan. Ed Sheeran tweeted simply, 'McBusted makes me happy.'

And, come 21 June at the Stade de France, McBusted made an entire stadium of fans very happy indeed.

As they were the support act for 1D, they couldn't bring their fancy set and flying cars with them, though. They did have the *Back to the Future* soundtrack still. How to make a show-stopping entrance without the car? Only McBusted could come up with this: tag-team leapfrog. Somehow apt for a concert staged in France.

The boys' union with 1D for the special gig set rumours aflame that perhaps a super-supergroup could be formed, with all three bands joining forces. Danny cheekily coined their potential name: 'McBust-erection'. And Tom declared to Magic FM, 'That's the only reason why we'd do it: for the comedy value of our name.'

But – in all seriousness – McBusted could only ever be McBusted. It could only ever be the six of them. James said of the group to the *Mirror*, 'It was like Lego. It just slotted together.' And Danny added, 'We're like a football team. There's no star player.'

There were just six stars.

Backstage on the tour, the band kicked back, chatting and relaxing as they made a vodcast for their devoted fans. When Dougie and Tom commented that they'd worked out that they must have played '5 Colours in Her Hair' more than 10,000 times in their career, it got James thinking. He did some quick calculations on his iPhone, then announced to the group that they had only 26 million minutes left to live.

McBusted planned to make every single one of them count.

Matt put it best to *Chronicle Live* when he said, 'This is the start of the future, you know. We never thought it would be this big . . . so everything we're doing now is already part of the future.'

As the McBusted mega-tour drew to a close, there was a knock on the door of their dressing room. In came the band's management, with a present for each of the musicians. It was a special plaque, commemorating the fact that

This is the start of the future

they'd sold out every single one of their arena dates, and entertained countless thousands of people along the way.

James held his almost reverentially in his hands. He spoke softly, amid the exclamations of his bandmates around him. 'This is the most special thing I've ever been given,' he said. 'I never thought I'd get something like this ever again.'

He looked around the room at his bandmates. It was Tom who had once said, on a VT at the Royal Albert Hall, 'Bandmates is different to just friends and best friends. It's closer to being brothers.' A new family had been fashioned from Busted and McFly – and, as Danny put it, 'When you have that [bond], you believe you can go on for ever.'

Harry got the last word, speaking to a fan about the supergroup.

When it comes to McBusted, he said simply, 'I do believe it's fate.'

Epilogue

McBusted had called a press conference.

It was becoming a bit of a habit.

And they had an enormous announcement to make.

The supergroup had been selected to headline the Barclaycard British Summer Time Festival in Hyde Park. They would be playing to 65,000 fans – more than three times the size of the O2 in London, the biggest arena on

> **This is going to be the biggest show of our lives**

their tour. This was a stage that the Rolling Stones had played, that Bruce Springsteen himself had rocked out on. It was the capital's biggest summer festival. And they were getting top billing.

As Tom put it on the McBusted YouTube channel, in a video made to announce the gig, 'This is going to be the biggest show of our lives. It's going to be the biggest show we've ever played. Potentially the biggest show we will ever play.'

Harry and Danny summed up the band's reaction by restaging the moment they were told.

Harry: 'You've been offered Hyde Park.'

Danny: 'What? Where's the [candid] camera?'

James added to *Good Morning Britain*, '[We] know how special this is. [Looking back] over the last ten years, you know what the special moments were. And you compare this to those special moments, and this is up there with those special moments – that maybe you didn't understand the first time round.' Danny agreed, with the wisdom of a decade in the business: 'You learn how to appreciate it.'

At lunchtime one day, the band were chilling out when they received news of who would be supporting them for the huge gig. Harry just managed to get his phone out in time to capture James's exuberant reaction. And it was James who had the honour of making the 'big reveal' of the support act at the press conference.

'We have a very special guest band at the event who will be playing,' he began, the excitement plain in his voice – and in his next statement. 'The idea that they're going to be playing . . . that is a whole dream come true in itself. It's the Backstreet Boys. I love the Backstreet Boys!'

And in fact, there couldn't have been a more apt choice for the supergroup. James, who had always been a fan of the Backstreet Boys' superbly crafted pop songs, had introduced Matt to their music when the two had first started working together, back in that historic springtime in Southend. The first song Tom had learned to play on piano was a Backstreet Boys song – a skill he later demonstrated in his original audition for Busted. And on that fateful day when Tom and Danny had first met, during Danny's dance-tastic boy-band audition for V, it was a Backstreet Boys track that Tom had taught him how to sing. James, of course, had also written for the group – but it's one thing being an anonymous songwriter, and another being the headlining act at a gig where your favourite band are supporting your own.

It was no wonder that, as applause at the news rippled around the press-conference room from the cynical media hacks, James jumped up and down and said, 'I'm going to clap too 'cause I'm excited!'

It was such an extraordinary turnaround for Matt and James – something Harry was conscious of. He said to James as they announced the news to the media, 'James, what would you have said if someone had said to you in the Busted press conference when you were splitting up, "Dude, don't worry, 'cause in eight, nine years, you're going to be headlining Hyde Park and the Backstreet Boys will be supporting you."?'

James didn't miss a beat. 'I would have said … quit playing games with my heart.'

The band threw themselves into rehearsals with gusto. And their minds turned, too, to what might be on the agenda for them after Hyde Park. They'd had interest from international promoters about taking the tour abroad – and the band were keen to explore the idea. James said enthusiastically, 'I would like to travel, and see places again.'

A journalist asked them if *McBusted: The Musical* might be on the cards. The band looked up and down their line-up. There was Matt, who had wowed the West End in *Wicked* and *Flashdance*; Danny, who had played guitar for his school's musical productions;

Dougie, who'd attended a performing-arts college; James, who had written an Olivier Award-nominated West End musical and two others besides, as well as playing Oliver at the London Palladium. Tom loved musicals so much that, for McFly's tenth-anniversary gigs, he'd actually penned an original ten-minute composition called *McFly: The Musical*. It seemed as if Matt was understating it when he replied, 'We are partial to a jazz hand.'

Tom said eagerly that the idea of *McBusted: The Musical* would be 'awesome', but James gave him a reality check from his own experience: 'I would love to but those things take so much time,' he said. He added, though, 'It's a really great idea . . .'

Perhaps it was something for Tom to jot down in those notebooks of his.

Speaking of books, he and Dougie certainly had a bright literary future ahead of them. Almost unexpectedly, they had become huge stars of the children's book world, writing a series of books about a diarrhoeic dinosaur. *The Dinosaur That Pooped Christmas* had been a surprise hit for Random House Children's Books in winter 2012; they'd followed it up with *The Dinosaur That Pooped a Planet*; and now they had a multi-book deal for more to come. They said bemusedly to Fearne Cotton, 'It was a joke that became a reality.' And Tom's publishers were in boosted-profile heaven when he won the Marvel Celebrity Dad of the Year Award, just three months after Buzz's birth.

It was a prize that caused a bit of a kerfuffle within the band, when Andi Peters asked Matt about Tom's win on *Good Morning Britain*. Dad-of-two Matt joked, 'I wasn't even nominated . . . I'm a terrible father.'

A terrible idea was a McBusted perfume. Yet, as the boys

exchanged sweaty trainers backstage on a McBusted vodcast, inhaling the inner sole, it was one James thought had potential. Of the boys' cheesy footwear scents, he said firmly, 'If that was a range, it would sell.'

The sky seemed the limit. Matt said to Fearne Cotton, 'In McBusted, we've been in this amazing position where we can just go, "Awesome." Whenever something comes up, we're like, "Do you want to do that?" We're like, "Yeah!"'

As ever, though, what they were really psyched about was making music together. Dougie gave hope to millions of fans when he told the *Daily Record* in July, 'There might be a McBusted album for Christmas, if we can get it done in time.' He explained, 'McFly had an album ready to go, but ... then we were like, "Sod it, let's do McBusted instead." So we might use some songs from that, and Matt and James have been writing ever since McBusted formed, so there's lots to choose from.'

And Harry added to the *Belfast Telegraph*, '[Recording] will happen after the tour. We'll be writing on the road and hopefully soon after the tour we'll get in the studio.' The dates had already been booked.

There might be a McBusted album for Christmas

But before all that was the small matter of the biggest gig of their lives. Danny said to Magic FM, 'It's still not sunk in really that we're headlining this, and how big it is.' Dougie added to Fun Kids, 'We're pee-your-pants excited.'

For Danny, too, there was the added thrill that this was a venue Springsteen had played. He said to Enas Refaei, 'I'm still in my own world that I'm actually going to stand and play on the same stage that Bruce Springsteen played. I might be in the same dressing room – so I might even smell the chairs and things!'

And the proximity of the Backstreet Boys was causing excitement, too. They supported McBusted at another gig a few days before the big one on Sunday, 6 July, and Tom revealed to Magic FM, 'We all stood side of stage and were fangirls over them. We knew all the words to every song.'

Tom was feeling moved about Hyde Park because of its incredible location in terms of McBusted's past. He said to Magic, 'This is an important place for us. We can almost see from the stage where we wrote most of McFly's first album [at the InterContinental], where we stayed when we were trying to get record deals . . . it's walking distance from the stage. This is where a lot of McFly and Busted history was born.'

Everyone wanted to know if they were going to be nervous, come Sunday. Danny said simply to *London Live*, 'We always play shows like it's the last show we'll ever play. We've got to look at it as any other show, go into it with as much energy as we do every time – but then remember that it is special. No matter how big it is, all the way to the back, we're gonna try and make everyone have the best time ever.'

And Tom chipped in with, 'You will see six very overly excited, hyperactive guys onstage on Sunday.'

Danny's words struck a chord with his bandmates, though, because the Hyde Park gig was the last show McBusted had in their schedule. Tom said to Magic FM, 'Hyde Park is the last show we have booked. We don't have any more McBusted shows planned for the future yet. Who knows what's going to happen?

'We're writing songs together and we love being McBusted and we genuinely get excited about the idea of having an album and doing more touring ... but who knows?'

For now, as he put it to The Vault, 'We are riding the wave of McBusted.'

And they were ready to catch a big one. Sunday, 6 July, dawned bright and clear – a perfect summer's day in the city. And McBusted made their way backstage.

They were in reflective spirit.

James said to Enas Refaei, 'We have a chance to create memories together.' Harry: 'We're super-proud of it all.'

As for Tom, he simply said, 'Hyde Park will be the most incredible moment of our careers.'

We are riding the wave of McBusted

In the dressing room, the sextet were warming up. There was Matt, jumping around like a maniac, buzzing on caffeine and anticipation. There was Danny, crying like a dog ('It's a good vocal warm-up,' he explained to Andi Peters). There was Harry, merrily doing press-ups to get his arms loosened for the pounding he would be giving his drums.

And where was James? Still making his way down from cloud nine, having just performed 'I Want It That Way' with the Backstreet Boys onstage. He later tweeted, 'Anyone who says dreams don't come true is telling a serious lie. Crossing this off my bucket list now: singing "I Want It That Way" with the Backstreet Boys.'

And then it was almost time for a show of their own. They gathered in a circle for 'the clap' of togetherness. The six of them, squeezed into one room. James said to *Good Morning Britain*, 'We don't have individual rooms or individual riders. We arrive together, we get changed together, we eat together, we shower together.'

And they played music together.

McBusted burst onto the stage with their usual energy. The crowd gave it back to them in spades. Playing to 65,000 people is an experience very few will ever have. James, Danny, Tom, Harry, Dougie and Matt were six of them.

Matt summed it up best. He said gloriously to the crowd, 'You have no idea how much this means . . . we can't believe we're playing here.'

And when, onstage, Dougie said sadly that he didn't ever want to leave, and suggested to the group that they start again from the very beginning, he could have been talking about the band itself. It was only the beginning for McBusted. And so they played on.

Harry was on the drums, the Uppingham boy who joined a band with only eighteen months' experience. He'd gone on to excel not only behind his kit, but on the dance floor too – and in love. He and Izzy were the happiest they'd ever been. And Harry said shyly to The Vault, 'Will there be a second McFly baby? I think at some point there will be; we'd hope.'

Playing along with his 'father figure', his best mate, his brother, was little Dougie Poynter. From the shy boy who wouldn't say boo to a goose, he had come a long way. It had been a rocky road, but he'd come out the other side. It said everything when Ellie Goulding, who was lovingly cheering him on in the crowd, tweeted a picture of her boyfriend up onstage, accompanied by just two words: 'Very proud.'

Danny was centre stage as usual, playing on the same stage as his hero Springsteen. Had you told the Bolton boy that one day he'd be up there, handling his guitar with all the speed and dexterity one might a cherry-red Porsche, he would never have believed you. In nine days' time, he and the McBusted boys would be heading to Ibiza for his stag do. The wedding was only weeks away now. Danny Jones was settling down at last.

Somehow, it felt even more satisfying than his wild days as a single man.

Tom, for one, was happily married, besotted with both Giovanna and his new baby Buzz. He said of Gi on *All Star Mr & Mrs*, 'Cheesy as it sounds, I think we were destined to be together.' And that wasn't the only thing that was meant to be in his life. Like all his bandmates, Tom Fletcher was an extremely talented man. When he'd cried in his bedroom all those years ago, after getting the boot from Busted, he could never have known that one day he would be headlining Hyde Park, singing songs that he'd written not only for his own band, but for his best friends, too.

But it was written in his stars, just as clearly as his love for Gi.

Matt and Emma were still going strong, too. Just the day before, they'd celebrated their sixth wedding anniversary. Emma had tweeted, 'At this time, six years ago today, @mattjwillis and I were married! I was 45 minutes late . . . Thanks for waiting babe. You are my world.' And Matt responded in kind, 'This day six years ago I became officially the luckiest man on earth and married the hottest girl I'd ever met! I love her more every day.'

Matt – as well as being a romantic – was still a joker. He still had that charisma that had landed him musical-theatre roles and those early comparisons to Robbie Williams. These days, he did it all without the buffer of booze, which made it even more impressive. He ran his fingers down his bass, and the crowd screamed. The showman was back onstage, where he belonged.

As was his bandmate, James Bourne. The boy who'd dreamed in Southend-on-Sea of a band to rock his world. Who'd had it all – and lost it all. He said on The Vault, 'McBusted has changed our lives. It's life-changing.' He'd returned to his home country in a literal blaze of glory, the scorched tyre tracks of the DeLorean still burning bright against the summer sky in Hyde Park.

'Do you feel like you've been given a second chance at it now?' he was asked on The Vault.

He paused thoughtfully. 'Yeah,' he said emphatically. 'A second chance at life.'

The showman was back onstage where he belonged

At the press conference to announce the supergroup, Harry had said, 'We're so lucky that we all get on so well. It's literally as simple as that. People are like, "What's your secret?"

'It's just that we find each other funny and we get on well – and we don't really ever argue. We'll have debates, and that's about it. I don't get bored of them.'

And it looked like the world wasn't getting bored of McBusted any time soon.

As they launched into '5 Colours in Her Hair' – for the ten-thousand-and-first time in Tom and Dougie's careers – the light shower that had dusted the park cleared to beautiful sunshine.

And a rainbow of five colours arched above the supergroup on their super stage.

Somewhere over the rainbow . . . dreams come true.

Author's Acknowledgements

First and foremost, I want to thank my husband – my first reader and my first love – who not only encouraged me to write this book in the first place, but kept me fed and watered and was a brilliant sounding board throughout the intense writing process. Thank you, darling.

Thanks too to my family and friends, who were almost as excited as I was about the fact I was writing a book all about my favourite band, and whose pride and enthusiasm means more to me than they can know. They even manage to look interested when I display my intimate knowledge of McBusted at every social occasion – and that's true friendship.

Special thanks to my editor Abigail Bergstrom, who has been passionate and supportive of this book from the word go. Thanks also to the entire team at Simon & Schuster, who believed in the book and championed it to retailers and the media alike. I'm truly grateful.

I'm indebted to the many McBusted aficionados out there who maintain their fan forums and YouTube channels with such diligence, pride and care. These were an invaluable resource in writing the boys' story.

Finally, thanks to the boys themselves: McBusted. James, Matt, Tom, Danny, Harry and Dougie, your music has been the soundtrack to my life, and it has been such an enormous privilege to write this book about you all. I have loved it from start to finish – but not as much as I love the music you have all created over the past twelve years or so. I cannot wait to see what you do next. You deserve your future to be totally awesome.

I'll be cheering you on, every step of the way.

Jennifer Parker, 2014

Sources

Books

Busted by Busted (Virgin Books, 2003)

Busted on Tour: The Official Book by Peter Robinson (Virgin Books, 2004)

Unsaid Things: Our Story by McFly (Transworld, 2012)

Magazines

Attitude

Bella

Closer

Glamour

Hello!

HR

Kerrang!

Music Week

NME

OK!

Q

Self

Smash Hits

Sound on Sound

Sugar

Music

A Present for Everyone by Busted

Above the Noise by McFly

'Angels Walk Beside You'
by 88

Busted by Busted

'Crashed the Wedding' /
'Build Me Up Buttercup'
by Busted, feat. McFly

Don't Let It Go to Waste by
Matt Willis

'Five Colours in Her
Hair' / 'Lola' by McFly,
feat. Busted

'Love is on the Radio' by
McFly (McBusted mix)

Motion in the Ocean by
McFly

Radio:ACTIVE by McFly

Room on the 3rd Floor by
McFly

Volume 1 by Future Boy

Welcome to Loserville by Son
of Dork

Wonderland by McFly

Newspapers

Birmingham Mail

Bolton News

Chronicle Live

Daily Mail

Daily Record

Daily Star

Express

Guardian

Liverpool Echo

Metro

Mirror

Observer

Plymouth Herald

Telegraph

Somerset News

Sun

Sunday Mirror

West Briton

TV, video and radio

5 NewsTalk Live

All Star Mr & Mrs

America or Busted

*Ant & Dec's Saturday Night
Takeaway*

Daybreak

CD:UK

Children in Need

Fearne and McBusted

The Frank Skinner Show

Fun Kids

GMTV

Good Morning Britain

I'm a Celebrity

I'm a Celebrity Hall of Fame

SOURCES

The Jonathan Ross Show

London Live

Magic FM

The Making of
   Radio:ACTIVE

McBusted: The Birth

McBusted Vodcast

McFly, 10th Anniversary
   Concert: Live at the Royal
   Albert Hall

McFly on the Wall

Newsround Showbiz

Popstar to Operastar

Radio 1

Radio 5 Live

Showbiz 411

Steve Wright in the Afternoon

Strictly Come Dancing

Sunday Side Up

T4

This Morning

Up Close and Personal

The Vault

VJ Scorpio TV

Websites

AbsolutePunk.net

AllMusic.com

Bailii.org

BBC.co.uk

BustedOnline.org

Celebrity.Yahoo.com

CultureWatch.org

DreamMoods.com

DigitalSpy.co.uk

EDP24.com

EntertainmentWise.com

Facebook.com

FleckingRecords.co.uk

FutureBoy.com

GigWise.com

heatworld.com

HuffingtonPost.co.uk

JamesBourneBrasil.com

MusicOMH.com

PopJustice.com

PoynterSource.com

SetList.fm

Sing365.com

Sugarscape.com

TES.co.uk

Twitter.com

VirginMedia.com

Wunderground.com

YouTube.com

Photo Credits

The author and publishers would like to thank the following copyright-holders for permission to reproduce images in this book:

© Rex Features 1, 5, 6, 8, 9, 11, 12, 13, 14, 16, 17, 19, 20, 23, 24, 25, 26, 27, 28, 30, 32, 33

© Getty Images 2, 3, 4, 10, 15, 21, 22, 29, 31, 34, 35, 36

© Corbis 7, 18